EX
LIBRIS

Faith
Made Them
Champions

EDITED BY NORMAN VINCENT PEALE

Faith Made Them Champions

GUIDEPOSTS ASSOCIATES, INC.

Carmel, New York

TO OUR FRIENDS

Who, in the early days of Guideposts when the obstacles were many, stood by most loyally. To Lowell Thomas, one of Guideposts' founders (along with Eddie Rickenbacker, Branch Rickey, Stanley Kresge), who by radio helped rebuild our circulation list destroyed in the fire which levelled our plant in 1947; to the Readers Digest which also announced the fire and helped us re-locate our subscribers, and to our good friends Mr. and Mrs. DeWitt Wallace who loaned us equipment and saw to it that we had expert Digest technical advice and continued encouragement; to the Pawling Methodist Church which made temporary quarters available after the fire; to those generous and zealous thousands all over the country who gave and are giving financial support, prayer and enthusiasm; to the unique parade of authors who have given of themselves and their experiences to Guideposts to help their fellowman; and to the many who have worked voluntarily in their precious spare time in the drive to extend the circulation and spiritual influence of Guideposts Magazine . . . we gratefully dedicate this book.

THE GUIDEPOSTS STAFF

FOREWORD

FOR YEARS Guideposts Magazine has had many requests saying: "Why not a special book of stories by athletes, adventurers and other champions? It would be a book to inspire both young and old in this age of increasing juvenile delinquency. When you publish the book I'd like to have a copy and get copies for young people."

Faith Made them Champions is the timely answer to these many requests. When preparation began on this volume, the editors of Guideposts Magazine were amazed to discover how many great sporting figures had written stories for Guideposts—stories of thrilling accomplishments over unbelievable obstacles ... fascinating accounts of how the energizing force of creative spiritual living develops heroism and championship performances.

Powerful bodies and special skills are not enough to produce champions. No, not even will power and determination. We learn from these stories how important it is to be a "right thinker." Champions, it seems, have a sense of rhythm and harmony with the universe. I am convinced that there is a rhythmic flow in life which moves according to a master plan, and that this plan is not man-made but God-made. Those who achieve the greatest accomplishments all say that the strain, tension and friction resulting from "going against the grain" defeats them. Those who get in tune with the easy flow and harmony of life, however, become released. All their powers function like a well synchronized mechanism. They become champions.

In *Faith Made them Champions,* such sports experts as Branch Rickey and Red Barber tell from their own experience what qualities makes the difference between a good and a great performer. Other outstanding athletes, who reveal the spiritual techniques which have helped them, include Carl Erskine, Bob Feller, Otto Graham, Bob Mathias, "Babe" Zaharias, Florence Chadwick, Babe Ruth, Ben Hogan, and Bob Richards.

All champions, of course, are not in the field of sports. America is famous for stories of average people who rose to extraordinary achievements in many professions. These Horatio Alger stories include those of Roy Rogers, Perry Como, Marian Anderson, Joel McCrea. We have also given a section of this book to the famous prayer stories of both athletes and champions in other fields. Favorites include the stirring narrative of President Eisenhower's boyhood recovery through prayer, the epic of the Four Chaplains and the creation of Uncle Sam's prayer.

Here are true experiences of real people which will make you tingle with the possibility of your own accomplishment. These persons do not give vague preachments, but in simple language tell *how* they have achieved, often against great odds. In each case, God is at the center. Somewhere in this volume will be an experience that will reach to the very core of your own problem or defeat and show you how to rise above it.

Only a few of the stories chosen for this treasure-book of inspiration have appeared in previous Guideposts books (*Guideposts, New Guideposts* and *Guideposts Anthology*). But the source of all material, of course, is that stimulating magazine for all faiths, Guideposts, published at Carmel, New York.

It is our hope that in this book you will find a dynamic approach to life which, in some way, will show you how to raise your performance from average to good, or from good to excellent, or from excellent to superior.

That is what we are here on earth for—

NORMAN VINCENT PEALE
Editor-in-chief

HOW TO USE
THIS BOOK

THE MOST strategic place for this book is in the home. Use it with daily devotions, selecting one story that may particularly fill your need. Many parents will want to read one story to their youngsters in the evening.

Mark those articles which will serve as speech illustrations and discussion topics; also any stories which may spark a new community project or help revive an old one. If possible, make the book available to your Sunday school and public school teachers; think of the innumerable people you can help by supplying a copy for your doctor's and dentist's office, the local hospital and library.

If you feel depressed or defeated, select one article that suits your mood. Read it carefully, visualizing how it might apply to your own situation. Picture yourself as coming into contact with all the rhythmic forces of the universe. Close your eyes and repeat: "They that wait upon the Lord shall renew their strength; they shall mount up with wings as eagles; they shall run, and not be weary; and they shall walk, and not faint." (Isaiah 40:31)

CONTENTS

HOW FAITH ATTITUDES
INSPIRE THE CHAMPION

SEVEN GREAT COMEBACKS

THESE MEN FOUND ADVENTURE

EXTRAORDINARY PROJECTS
OF ORDINARY YOUTH

WHAT CAN HAPPEN THROUGH PRAYER

SPECIALISTS IN OVERCOMING OBSTACLES

WHAT

MAKES A

GOOD

PERFORMER

GREAT

PAGE 31

PAGE 27

PAGE 7

PAGE 15

PAGE 24

PAGE 2

WHAT MAKES
THE DIFFERENCE

by BRANCH RICKEY

The great Ty Cobb once turned a base-on-balls into a home run. But another player hit a real "homer" only to be thrown out at third base. What made the difference between champ and chump? Branch Rickey, the famous developer of baseball talent, gives you his 3-way system to help an average boy become a real star.

BASEBALL is my business, but it is much more than that. I still get the same thrill out of the game I did as a kid. In our Pittsburgh organization today there are nearly 400 players, most of whom I know personally, as well as many of their fathers, mothers, sisters, brothers, aunts and uncles.

I'm no father to these boys—they don't want that. I am their employer, and they have to make good. But I also want to be their friend and will do everything I can to help them.

These players have ability—all of them. Many will play in the Major Leagues if they perform up to their capacities. It is my job, and that of our managers and coaches, to bring men to their best—*to help make ability and capacity meet.*

Some of the players will come through. Others won't.

What makes the difference?

There are three qualities which seem to me to be highly valuable, if not indispensable, to success.

First, a man should feel that the job he is doing is worthwhile. A man can sell something better if he believes in it. The fact that the product is worthwhile dignifies his efforts; he is continuously challenged to do better.

Perhaps there are some who feel that baseball shouldn't occupy the important place that it does today in the life of our people. Yet how a nation acts on its play-fields—and at its diversions— gives an accurate picture of the character of its people.

The United States is a sports-loving and sports-indulging nation. Over 20,000,000 boys follow the records of great athletes closely and find many heroes to worship in the professional game. The press, radio and television daily give wide coverage to contests. Since baseball is such a permanent enterprise, responsible folk must give close attention to the health of this sport.

It is simply great, therefore, if a ball player believes that what he is doing has purpose and dignity and is worthwhile.

The second point is even more important, and is best illustrated by two contrasting stories . . .

Many years ago, when I was managing the St. Louis Browns, I lost a game to Detroit in the last half of the eleventh inning in a very unusual manner—nothing else like it in the record books anywhere. Detroit came to bat in the last half of the eleventh inning in a tie-score game, two men out and nobody on the bases, when a player named Ty Cobb came to bat.

Cobb got a base on balls and then scored the winning run without another ball being pitched. By sheer adventure and skill he forced two wild throws by St. Louis infielders. His daring at first base, his boldness and skillful turn at second, his characteristic slide ten feet before he reached third, his quick coordination following his slide—all brought about four "breaks" in his favor. He made what amounted to a home run out of a base on balls.

In the very same game, there was a player on my team by the name of Walker, a man who had all the physical qualities to be a great player. During a game in Beaumont, Texas, the following spring, Walker hit what should have been a home run—and was thrown out at third.

Walker's slow start to first base, as he watched his hard line drive fall between the left and center fielders, cost him 20 feet. Next, he lost another 30 feet making too wide a turn around first toward second base. Then, seeing the elusive ball on its way to the Texas prairies (the left field fence was down for repair), he slowed to a jog trot. This easily cost him still another 50 feet, and he was now 100 feet behind schedule.

Suddenly the ball struck some object, a board or stone, and bounced back into the hands of the surprised center-fielder, a boy by the name of Al Nixon. Nixon's quick turn and his strong arm brought the throw toward third. Walker, seeing that a play could now be made on him, put on a great burst of speed. He made a fall-away slide to the right and into the very hands of the third baseman. Walker actually tagged himself out.

Exclamatory groans came from our bench. One chap in disgust kicked over the water bucket, and another threw a bunch of bats helter-skelter into the air.

In discussing the play later, however, everyone agreed that if Walker had not made any one of four mistakes—the slow start from home plate, the wide turn at first, the walking trot around second, and the slide to the wrong side at third—there could have been no play upon him. And if he had made all four correctly, he would have scored a home run standing up.

What is the difference between Cobb and Walker? They had about the same age, weight, height, and running speed. Walker had a stronger arm than Cobb and more power at the bat. Yet one rose to unparalleled fame; the other lives in obscurity. Cobb wanted to do something so much that nothing else mattered; Walker punched the clock.

A consuming desire to be great is *the important second quality* that will help make ability and capacity meet. This desire can turn a faulty, youthful hitter like Enos Slaughter into a great batsman. It can produce a good base runner out of a slow runner. The greatest single factor that makes a championship player is his *desire* to be one, and the greatest quality of a championship club is a collective, dominating urge to win.

Luck? Yes, there is luck in all athletic contests, due to causes we don't control and cannot anticipate. Usually, good luck is the by-product of planned effort. Bad luck will feature any club which is satisfied with mediocrity. A man who has the bad habit of looking at his batted ball, which he can no longer direct, or follows a course that carries him 30 feet too far, or assumes victory before he has it, shouldn't charge his failure to "bad luck."

Baseball clubs can have injuries and illnesses and military drafts and "bad breaks," but I think these should be regarded as merely incidents on a highway of progress.

The greatest devotion to high purpose that I know anything about was exemplified in the Life of a Man who died 2,000 years ago. And He lived only 33 years. It is significant to me that when Jesus was only 12 years of age, He so knew His direction and purpose that He could say to inquiring parents, and respectfully too: "Wist ye not that I must be about my Father's business?" *

In common parlance, Christ had many bad "breaks"—born in a barn; crucified in the open between two thieves; and during His life many others. Yet He left a religion which—if believed in and followed with devotion—could solve personal, community and international ills.

There is a third quality which makes a difference in men . . .

I have seen many players who have had the material requisites for greatness—youth, size, speed, power, and even desire—and yet fail utterly. Such cases are tragic, indeed, where the boy wants to be great, his people counting upon him, and yet he cannot *master the little skills which go with excellence.* He cannot learn to hold men on base, or he cannot slide, or he over-

* *Luke 2: 49*

strides at bat, or he cannot get a proper lead. There are a hundred so-called "little" things that mark the difference between the ordinary and the exceptional.

I like to go into a dentist's office where the magazines are current. Somehow, I anticipate newer techniques, better treatment. I like to go into a church of any faith, where the builders have had in mind a beautiful edifice. Not elaborate necessarily, but with attention to detail. Once inside, the pews, the chancel, the pulpit, the choir loft, the organ and the windows—all and everything—seeming to combine to produce a sense of worship, even without music or without a word being said to anybody. I like that. You can feel at once that you are in a place where you are already getting what you need—spiritual medicine.

I like players who are masters of detail in their work. Men acquiring these little skills please everybody and "sell" themselves. They make good.

I shall be very happy when the time comes in Pittsburgh that we have boys who, first of all, feel that they are doing something worthwhile. Second, as gentlemen, they want to win a pennant so much that they never ask the price, but pay it. And, third, I shall be gratified beyond expression if they are skilled, real masters of technique, both on offense and on defense. For then, the Pittsburgh Club will be highly rated in the National League and they won't scare in the World Series.

Illustration, Branch Rickey and Pittsburgh players, see page 1

HIGH ABOVE
THE CENTER RING

by F. BEVERLY KELLEY

*What kind of people are circus people? What group
of performers had the most remarkable escape from
disaster of all time? Beverly Kelley, advance man
for Ringling Bros., Barnum & Bailey Circus, gives
some dramatic sketches of an exciting business.*

A FRIEND and I were watching the 1954 edition of the circus
when it opened in New York's Madison Square Garden. The
stars were doing their stuff before an enthusiastic audience.
Interwoven with adult applause was the extra accolade that
circus people prize above all else: the bell-like quality of child
laughter that keeps ringing in the memories of old troupers
when the leotards and the motley have been hung up in retire-
ment. For the circus is for the young in years and the young in
heart.

"What kind of people are circus people?" my friend asked
me.

"Just people," I replied—"good and bad and in-between like
the folks in any town. The circus is a traveling town that builds
a new home in a new town every day—maybe a hundred and
fifty different cities in an eight-month tour."

Then I realized that I had sold them short. Really they are
very special people. One of the ways in which they are special
is their tolerance and general good nature. Ringling Bros. and
Barnum & Bailey has more than a thousand traveling personnel.
They come from the ends of the earth—all creeds, colors, na-
tionalities.

They work hard and they work together. It is difficult to hate
anyone you work beside and whose ability and courage you

7

respect. In the outdoor show business you fight elemental things: time and space and weather and danger, instead of each other. I don't think you could ever start a war if you had to start it among circus people.

They come from all over the world, and a lot of them make mighty good Americans. I'm thinking of a family of flying trapezists named Otari. They were born in Russia, came to the U.S.A. about twenty years ago and took out their citizenship papers. When World War II came, the four boys enlisted and went away, breaking up the act. One was killed on the Normandy beach head.

When the war was over and the act was put together again, the sixty-year-old father of the family went back up into the rigging to replace the son who had died for his adopted country. Amy Porter of *Collier's* wrote a story about him and called him the "Daring *Old* Man On The Flying Trapeze."

The reason I am recounting this story about the Otaris is because the boy who died on D-Day had written a letter to his family and had said, "I used to wonder why in our business they always said, 'the show must go on.' Sometimes it didn't make much sense. But now I'm with a 'show' that *must* go on, and I'm proud to be with it."

Circus people by tradition are supposed to be superstitious. I know a high-wire artist named Karl Wallenda who had a "lucky" ring that was given to him in his youth by a retired German performer. When held to the light, you could discern in the ring, inside a gem, the tiny figure of a high-wire walker, balancing pole and all.

Karl wore this ring at all times and he had it on the night the troupe fell in Akron, Ohio. The cable was guyed out to a "mud block" outside the tent and a wagon caught a wheel spoke in it and jiggled it just enough to upset the delicate equilibrium of the four Wallendas while they were executing their spectacular finish trick—a three-high human pyramid.

They toppled. There was no net. Two of the family managed to catch their hocks on the cable and hung on. Karl grabbed the cable with his hands and, hanging down, caught Helen between his legs, scissor-fashion, as she went past him toward the ground forty feet below.

This particular escape from disaster was the most remarkable of all time.

"After the Akron accident I began to put too much confidence in that 'lucky' ring," Karl recalls. "In fact, I was afraid to go up without it. Then one day during an ocean swimming party I lost it in the sand. At first I was panic-stricken. Then I realized that I had been putting my trust in superstition instead of in God. When I had added it up that way, I was glad I'd lost it; I haven't fallen since."

We watched a beautiful young woman named Josephine Berosini working alone on the high wire. She has five generations of circus people behind her. Josephine told me once of a day in Oklahoma City some years ago when a bicycle, on which the Berosini family had mounted a human pyramid, broke down sixty feet above the ground. It happened during the State Fair.

The pyramid was supposed to roll on the bicycle to the safety of the opposite end of the wire, where the platform was. With the vehicle unable to move, however, they were stuck there in mid-air. The top-mounter, Josephine's sister, could not descend from her father's shoulders without putting her foot in front of her father's face. If his vision of the wire was obscured, he could not balance and he was the understander of the whole three-high pyramid.

All this while, officials of the Fair were calling to the fire department to come with ladders and nets.

"It was only ten or fifteen minutes," Josephine remembers, "but that's a long time to hold a family on your shoulders and it seemed like years to us. We thought we were all going down.

"We talked about the wonderful times we had had together

and how much we loved each other, and we prepared for death. Then we started praying. Praying somehow gave us a new hope, and we decided we could try once more to get my sis off Dad's shoulders. 'Do it very quickly, take a chance,' my father ordered; 'this time we have God up here with us.'

"My sister came down so fast that Dad didn't have to take his eyes off the cable for more than a couple of seconds. We swayed, but we didn't fall. With sis off Dad's shoulders, the rest was comparatively easy and we all made it."

Circus people I have admired have a quiet, unpretentious kind of faith, which has its genesis in ability and upon a real working relationship with a Higher Power. They have what a person of small faith might call a fatalistic philosophy. But I think that what they have, instead, is a solid and relaxed feeling when they are tempting fate. They are gamblers by nature of their defiance of such inescapable forces as gravity. They scarcely expect a patient Providence to protect them if they make foolish mistakes that run contrary to their training as professionals. But they feel that so long as they do their best they may expect God's love and protection as may people in less hazardous pursuits.

Next time you're at the circus, watch them before they climb— how they pause to look up.

Illustration, Beverly Kelley, see page 1

SHE EARNS
FOR THOSE WHO CAN'T

by **LEN LE SOURD**

A beautiful young champion has a unique way of helping others.

HER FATHER was nearly buried alive on a battlefield!

It was World War I, and young Clyde R. Scott, an eager lad of seventeen, upped his age a few years to join the Canadian Army. In the Battle of Ypres a shell tore through him, taking along half his hip.

After the battle, weary, red-eyed German stretcher-bearers stumbled over his inert body. Thinking him dead, they dumped him with other corpses and wheeled him toward the burial grounds.

"Luckily some young soldier heard my father moan," Barbara Ann recalls. Burial was that close!

Young Scott was removed to a prison hospital, later survived almost five years of prison camp. Eventually, he returned to his beloved Canada, married and became Military Secretary to the Canadian Department of National Defense. Three children were born: Bill, Mary, and finally Barbara Ann in 1928.

The Scotts lived in Sandy Hill, just outside of Ottawa. Their house was situated on a bluff overlooking the Rideau River in a knot of homes belonging to military personnel. Community life was closely knit about the church. Barbara's grandfather had been a minister, and the family emphasized religious principles which had given dignity and purpose to generations of Scotts.

Because of war injuries, Colonel Scott couldn't bend down to tie his shoes. This plagued him for years. Finally, he became so irritated at the inconvenience that he devised a special pole with a hook to solve the problem.

"See!" he said triumphantly to his adoring daughter. "You can overcome anything if you keep at it."

"My father had everything—love, courage, faith," Barbara states proudly. "I never knew him to go back on his word. He'd keep going sometimes when he was half dead, yet he always had time to listen to someone else's troubles."

Barbara herself began to shake off ailments at the age of two when a tormenting pain in her ear made it necessary to open it eight times. In later years she went through skating performances despite temperatures, measles, and once a cracked hip.

Shortly before Christmas in 1932, Barbara, aged six, laboriously penned a note to Santa. "Dear Santa—a pair of one-runner skates fastened to boots, and a horse." Perhaps the last three words blurred before Santa, but he did leave her a pair of skates.

Mrs. Scott began to knit and sew skating clothes for her golden-haired daughter, who daily trudged down to Ottawa's Minto Skating Club to practice figure-skating. The 1936 Olympics had just pronounced Sonja Henie "Queen of Silver Skates." Barbara dreamed that someday she too might flash winged feet before audiences the world over.

At the age of ten, Barbara climaxed years of practice when she passed her gold medal tests for the Canadian Figure-Skating Association. She was the youngest on record to do this.

Beaming with success, she faced her trainer, a short Czech, kindly but a strict disciplinarian. His eyes gauged any newly acquired conceit. "Now we start and learn how to skate," he announced crisply. Barbara knew that he spoke the truth.

This period was one of frequent heartaches for the agile young skater and some perplexity for her parents. There was no driving ambition on *their* part for Barbara to develop into a great skater. In fact, her eagerness to learn resulted in frequent hardships, especially for Mrs. Scott, who spent many cold hours, with numbed feet, watching Barbara practice.

THE BALANCE WHEEL

by WALTER "RED" BARBER

*This nationally known sportscaster and columnist
tells what it takes to make a successful ball player.*

DISPOSITION IS certainly the balance wheel of a baseball player.

Physical assets in baseball, such as the ability to hit a ball hard, to throw a baseball swiftly and with accuracy, to run fast are all very necessary attributes. However, without a proper disposition, the athlete blessed with natural power will not make the grade in the Major Leagues. It is how a ball player thinks that is so vitally important.

In my years of announcing sports, I have become deeply impressed with the importance of disposition. Managers, club executives, coaches, and scouts are filled with the sad knowledge of so many physically gifted athletes who did not stand the wear of time and did not arrive at goals they should have reached because they lacked a good disposition. On the other hand, there are many Major League ball players who make the grade despite not having all the physical attainments because they make up their minds that they are going to succeed and they will not accept defeat.

Disposition means that a person is industrious—in baseball they call industriousness "hustle." This word "hustle" is the key word in baseball. It is the word that you hear every minute, every hour of the day at spring training camps. It is the word you hear all through the season. Managers demand hustle. They insist that ball players run out pop flies. They insist that a player hustle not for one, two, or three innings, but for nine or more innings, if necessary. They insist that a player hustle not for a week, but for the five and a half months that cover the regular season. They insist that outfielders run at top speed after everything hit their way. They insist that pitchers not let up. In fact, the disposition of a pitcher can often be most accurately measured by watching how he pitches when he is behind and is apparently pitching for a losing cause. Baseball scouts will not make up their minds on a young pitcher in the minor leagues until they see how he pitches when he is getting beat.

George Sisler told me several years ago that Ty Cobb was not a great natural hitter, but that Cobb had such a disposition to do as best he could, that he made himself the great hitter that he was. Cobb studied opposing pitchers. He studied all the opposing players; he studied himself; he changed his batting stance; he thought of ways to upset the opposition. If the other team played its infield deep, Cobb would bunt. When they pulled their infield in, then he hit. If they swung the outfield in one direction, he tried to hit to the opposite. His concentration on a winning performance was so steady, so relentless, that he was a man on fire. It was Cobb's disposition that made the great difference in this great player.

Connie Mack, venerable manager of the Philadelphia Athletics for so many years, has said that beyond doubt the great record of all baseball records was the number of batting titles that Cobb won. Cobb, in winning the American League batting crown twelve times, had to drive himself over a long period of years against constantly changing competition, against the times that he was hurt or sick, against bad weather, against all the factors that beset an individual performer.

It is much more difficult to remain on the top of the heap than it is to get there. In struggling for the top, the very horizons of something yet to be achieved are a tremendous incentive, but once those horizons have been crossed then it is a matter of standing off all those others who are reaching for top honors. And so in those years Cobb fought back against an understandable human lethargy that, but for the fiber of his disposition, would have brought him back among the pack.

Babe Pinelli, one of the best of umpires, is an exact case in this matter of personal disposition. When Pinelli was playing ball as a third baseman for Cincinnati, he was one of the most hotheaded and belligerent of players. He had a great number of fights, to say nothing of bitter arguments. As we say in sports, "Pinelli was ready." Then his playing days came to a close in the Pacific Coast League. He had a family and he liked baseball, and knew nothing else. He resolved that he would become an umpire, and he knew that he could not last a week as an umpire with the same disposition that he had possessed as a player—or better still, the disposition that had possessed him as a player. Pinelli made up his mind that he would curb his temper, that he would umpire with coolness, fairness, and with all the judicial patience that profession demands.

Pinelli has very little trouble with other ball players. He gives them a hearing when they have a squawk and then he says: "You've had your beef, now let's get back to the ball game." He is always equable and has gained the complete respect of the men with whom he associates. In addition to mastering his disposition, he yet continues to hustle on the playing field as an umpire, as he hustled as a ball player.

Dr. Jock Sutherland, one of our great football coaches, says that no matter what the physical ability of a man is, he cannot be a successful football player unless he has the disposition to be one. He must be of a frame of mind to want to play football, which means he must be willing and ready and eager to block, to tackle, to go through the long grueling hours of practice, which is the only way to bring about perfection of detail. A successful whole is only attained by perfection of detail.

It has been my experience to see repeatedly teams and individuals who would not be defeated. That meant that they paid the price of full practice, of strict training, of belief in their teammates, and in those others who guided their destiny. It is only from a man's disposition that he is empowered to go through each day's job and give it everything he possesses. It is only from a man's disposition that he gathers the strength to meet the stresses and crucial moments that come to all human beings. Weakness, as well as strength, stems from this trait, loosely known as "disposition." The faith we bring to anything is an evidence of our disposition. In a very real sense, the teachings in the Bible are inseparably tied with this matter of human disposition. On every page it is pointed out to those of us who read, that "For as he thinketh in his heart, so is he."

Illustration, Red Barber, see page 1

THE MARINE "APPLE POLISHER"

by BERT KESSEL

A misfit and weakling in training—a youth who read the Bible in his spare time—suddenly became a battlefield hero. Bert Kessel, who led his Marine company in the invasion of Iwo Jima, tells the stirring tale of "Squeaky."

MY FIRST introduction to Private Danny Forrest was at Hawaii. Here our Marine detachment was put through final combat training. Private Forrest, or "Squeaky" as he was called, was obviously a misfit.

As soon as Private Forrest opened his mouth all confusion regarding his nickname was cleared up. He had a falsetto voice. Squeaky was awkward, frail-looking—in fact everything a fighting Marine shouldn't be. He also bore the odious label of "eager beaver" (apple polisher).

Few Marines would have anything to do with him. When they did speak to him, it was derisively in high mock voices. Most irritating was Squeaky's efforts to court everyone's favor, both enlisted men and officers. Actually this was nothing more than an earnest attempt to be friendly—to be a good fellow— but no one bothered to look at it in this light.

In typical eager fashion Private Forrest had first applied for assignment to a machine gun crew. They made him a cook. Not that Squeaky might not have made a good machine gunner. But no one wanted him in his crew.

Along with Squeaky's desire to be a good fellow, was his very devout feeling for God. Much of his free time was spent reading the Bible. He even organized a weekly prayer meeting in his tent —but few could be induced to attend. Not discouraged, Squeaky continually forced his way into "bull sessions," then would "pipe up" with some religious application to the topic of discussion. His contributions were ignored.

It was unfortunate that Squeaky tried to be such a strong disciple of the Lord in this setting, because rather than build up, he tore down the vitality of religion in the eyes of many Marines. Under a strenuous mental and physical strain Marines looked to strength for their values, and Private Forrest and his religion somehow represented weakness.

Because I felt sorry for Squeaky and had been friendly to him on several occasions, he singled me out as a special friend. One day he approached me in great agitation. With rumpled hair and his face red with suppressed anger, Squeaky was struggling to keep back the tears.

"Lieutenant Kessel," he began, "will you teach me how to fight?"

"Why?" I asked, surprised.

"Because I . . ." Then angry tears began to fall and out poured his bitter story. One of the Marines, Private Brewster, had vented his irritation against Squeaky by giving him a physical drubbing. Brewster was a tower of a man, and I judged he could probably manhandle three or four like Squeaky at one time without greatly mussing up his hair. Squeaky's determination to learn to fight and avenge his beating was absurd, but I admired his spirit.

"Look," I said to him, "it won't do any good to mix it up with Brewster again. We've got a bigger job to do than to waste time fighting each other. Why don't you try to make Brewster your friend? You two may wind up in a fox-hole together before many weeks!"

I wasn't able to discover during the next weeks if Squeaky followed my advice. None of the men knew it at this time, but we were preparing to lead the assault on Iwo Jima. Indeed, it seemed only a few days after this particular incident when my unit stormed the beaches and began to fight inch by inch for the white dust that was Iwo.

Our casualties were terrific. My first glimpse of Squeaky amid the death and bloodshed was when he hurried by fastened to one end of a stretcher. His duties as a cook were so limited that he was doubling with the stretcher crew.

And casualties among stretcher bearers were especially high. Yet here was Squeaky, the so-called weakling, jumping up at every chance to take the place of wounded bearers. Men who had scorned and despised him during training looked at him now with new expressions. The savage fighting was producing many surprises. Several men, pillars of strength in training, had been pitiful failures under fire, while many of the "weak" ones were demonstrating high courage.

Squeaky was soon to perform even more spectacularly!

Fighting during the day was sheer carnage, but the nights in many ways were worse—because of the mental factor. For the Japs developed nasty habits of creeping furtively into our fox-holes and quietly slicing up our men while they dozed.

For three nights this happened. Something had to be done. Then Squeaky chimed in his suggestion.

"Lieutenant," he said, "I can see good at night. Station me in the advance fox-hole, and I'll spot the Japs before they get a chance to sneak in on us."

"Why not!" It sounded crazy, but anything was worth a try. Squeaky wasn't much use with a gun, but good eyesight was a much better weapon than a gun at night.

But Squeaky almost didn't have a chance to show his cat's vision. That day he stopped some mortar fragments in his arm. The wound wasn't serious, but I ordered him to return to the hospital for repairs.

Night had just begun to fall when to my surprise there was

Squeaky edging up to the advance fox-hole. I stopped him: "Forrest, I thought I ordered you out of action."

He displayed a bandage on his arm. "Look. Got it all fixed up."

The bandage was a sorry one. I shrugged my shoulders, concealing my admiration. The kid had real heart and I wasn't going to stop him from doing his stuff. I knew he had but one burning ambition—to show his fellow soldiers that he was every inch a Marine.

That night the Japs tried their infiltration tactics again. This time they didn't reckon with a slight, insignificant-looking Marine—with uncanny vision. The rest of us stared fixedly through the blackness, and saw nothing. Squeaky could see and did. He didn't dare speak out, but he could point. Then other Marines would blaze away with their rifles at shadowy lumps on the ground.

It was an unforgettable, eerie night. Many lives depending on the gestures of one man! Squeaky sometimes couldn't contain himself, and we could hear his excited whispers. Then suddenly it dawned on me who was with him in the fox-hole *Private Brewster!*

The next morning we counted dead Japs all around the area. Squeaky was a real hero, although nothing in the kidding friendly tones of his new buddies revealed the admiration they felt. Brewster had his arm about Squeaky, and the shining light in Squeaky's eyes told me more than any word could.

I never found out when Squeaky slept. During the days he carried stretchers, and at night he was indefatigable on watch. Once during a daytime lull I saw him reading the Bible instead of sleeping. His face was serene, almost happy. Now if he could have held his Bible sessions I think the whole Marine detachment would have attended. To the men Squeaky's religion was the answer to his amazing stamina and courage. They found themselves turning to religion for courage and strength.

By the fifteenth day our ranks had greatly thinned. Brewster had been killed, and I could see that his death touched Squeaky deeply. The two had become very close. Then it happened.

Squeaky was out with the stretchers as usual. Suddenly a mortar shell broke almost on top of him, and those nearby could almost feel the steel rip into flesh as Squeaky doubled up. Quickly he was placed on a stretcher, alive, but his stomach filled with mortar fragments. As Squeaky was carried away, his buddies looked on with blank, inscrutable expressions—mute testimony to their inner emotions. I had a lump in my throat the size of a melon.

At the end of the campaign I tallied up our losses. Of the original 260 men in my company who stormed the beaches the first day, about forty were left.

Several weeks later I received a letter from Squeaky. With much relief I read that he was out of danger. After reviewing his Iwo experiences, "a lifetime rolled into a few days," he called it, he asked about many of his buddies.

"In a way I am grateful to the Iwo campaign even though it was agony for us and death for so many swell guys," he wrote. "I found something there I had been looking for all my life."

I knew what he meant.

Squeaky's only request was that I send him his Bible and prayer material. As I fingered his religious possessions I thought of many things . . . his pitiful attempts to win friends at Hawaii . . . the amazing changes in so many men once they were under fire . . . the power of Squeaky's religion . . . the leadership it gave him. Many Marines had turned to religion on Iwo—in fear and desperation. Squeaky already had his "inner strength" when he arrived.

When I saw Squeaky praying he seemed to be thanking God for something already received. There was a great difference.

Illustration, Bert Kessel, see page 1

WHAT SPARKS THE SPEARHEAD?

by STONEY JACKSON

Otto Graham is the attacking spearhead of the Cleveland Browns Professional Football Club that has won championships five out of the last eight years. Four times he was named to the All-Pro team, twice was elected most valuable player in the league. No other player in professional football tops Otto Graham in all-round championship performance.

QUESTION: *Do you think professional football rates high for clean play?*

Graham: Pro football is no game for weaklings—everyone knows that. The men are rugged, they play hard, but they play clean. When men get into big time football, they're good enough not to have to play dirty. We love the game and we believe football competition, as well as all sports competition, makes high types of men.

Question: *How do you feel about Negroes and whites playing football together?*

Graham: Take Marion Motley, our big, powerful, 250-pound Negro fullback. When I hand off the ball to him and he goes plowing through the opposing line, he is beautiful. Or when he keeps those 200-pound enemy linemen off my back. He could be pink or purple and I would still love him. We haven't time, nor can we be bothered to consider a man's color, religion or background. All we ask is, "Can he play football?" Football is a great equalizer.

Question: *What builds such good team spirit among the Browns?*

Graham: Before each game, we hold a special meeting for

24

players in the dressing room. Nothing formal or fancy. We repeat the Lord's Prayer together. We don't pray for any special favors, just the prayer that Jesus taught His Disciples. We figure that whatever happens on the field will be the right thing.

We're not the only football team that does this. The Los Angeles Rams pray before games; so does Michigan State. Others do, I'm sure.

Question: *When did a personal faith become vital to you?*

Graham: Soon after our first child was born. Good as my early Christian training was, I took it pretty much for granted. My prayers were automatic. Since there were no real crises in my early life, I felt no dependence on anything but my own powers.

After my son, Duane, was born six years ago, I began to think seriously about the important things in life. I compared my life with others who had reached the top through sheer courage and perseverance—and with those who are still struggling and have little to show but disappointment and hardship. I was astounded to discover how fortunate and blessed I have been—why I do not know.

With this realization of my good fortune came, for the first time, a deep feeling of gratitude. I desired my son to have a sense of God in his life, realizing that he might not have as smooth going as I have had.

I saw clearly that my life has some definite reason and purpose back of it that human reason cannot explain. My wife, Beverly, and I then decided that all our children would be given the best opportunities in religious training—that we would be conscious at all times of our obligation to God and of our need for Him.

Today we go to the Methodist Church in Bay Village, Ohio, a Cleveland suburb where we live. We selected this church because it ties in best with our family program. To me, it isn't the label outside of your religion that counts, but the quality inside.

Question: *Have you ever had any unusual answer to prayer?*

Graham: Yes, and I hesitate to relate it. We follow a general rule that it isn't right to pray to win—but on one occasion I never prayed more fervently to win in my life.

It happened during the final championship game with the Los Angeles Rams, two years ago. We had only minutes to play, the Rams led us 28–27. Then, on a crucial play, I fumbled the ball.

Our defensive line-up went in, but with so little time left it looked hopeless for us. I went back to the bench, and unashamedly prayed that somehow Cleveland wouldn't lose because of my blunder.

No sooner had I finished my prayer than our defensive team held the Rams for downs, and they were forced to kick. I went back in as we took over on our 16-yard line, seconds and 84 yards away from the Los Angeles goal. I faked a pass, and got loose for 15 yards, running out of bounds to stop the clock. Two passes clicked for 14 and 18 yards. Our line opened up another nice hole, through which I went for another ten yards.

The clock was running out, so our place-kicking specialist, Lou Groza, came in. Lou booted the ball between the goal posts as the gun sounded, giving us a last-minute 30-28 victory.

I don't think that God gave us the breaks in this game because of mine or anyone else's prayer. But I know that I was dead tired when I came back to the bench after that fumble. After my prayer, somewhere I had picked up new energy.

This much I know for certain. I give God complete credit for the wonderful life I've had. I believe prayer is the key to successful living and I want my children to grow up with that knowledge.

Illustration, Otto Graham, see page 1

MY FRIEND ZASU

by FRANCES MARION

The beloved star, Zasu Pitts, learned to overcome a personality hazard at an early age. Her best friend, the noted scenarist and novelist, tells all about it.

WHEN ZASU PITTS was thirteen, that tormenting age between childhood and adolescence, she was shy, awkward, and scrawny. Her mother, a widow with several children to support, rented rooms to summer visitors who flocked into the little Western seaport town of Santa Cruz, California. Zasu helped her with the cooking, scrubbing, and washing.

No "chums" ever walked to school with Zasu, for she was the girl from the other side of the railroad tracks, who wore hand-me-downs, and who could *never* give a party. She could join no after-school activities because loyalty demanded she help her mother. Zasu's middle names are Loyalty and Dependability. The boys sent her comic valentines. They pulled her pigtails and made fun of her name ... "Boo-hoo, Za-su ... monkey face, from a zoo!"

But no one ever saw tears in Zasu's eyes, not even her mother. She walked alone, and she wept alone. But she wept a lot. Few little girls were as lonely or out of things.

Being one of those little girls who dream mighty dreams to escape from the sting of ridicule, Zasu lived in the half-world of illusion. She saw herself in a dotted swiss dress, not the old faded cotton trimmed with rickrack which had been made over from one of her mother's. She saw herself surrounded by admiring chums, and the recipient of lacy valentines from boys. She went home each day, not to the shabby cottage that needed a coat of paint, but to a stately house with iron deer on the lawn.

The most exciting dream, however, was when she visualized herself upon the platform in the auditorium at school, dramatically reciting "The Midnight Ride of Paul Revere." She heard the burst of applause! Saw herself stepping off the platform with an indifferent shrug of her shoulders. Let them run after her! Let them curry favors! A great tragedienne can pick and choose!

One afternoon, as Zasu walked home alone, swinging her school books on a long strap, a pebble struck her cheek. Voices rose from behind the fence. "Boo-hoo, Za-su . . . monkey face from a zoo!"

A group of girls passing by giggled as boys formed a taunting circle around her. For a moment, Zasu wanted to throw herself upon the ground and sob. Then shades of her Irish ancestors whooshed to her protection. "I'll lick every one of you!" she yelled.

"Dare you to!"

Before you could say "Be a lady," she had sailed into them, fists and fingernails, good strong teeth and double-soled shoes.

"What's going on here?" a voice thundered. It was the Principal of the school!

In a flash, all the mice had fled to their holes but Zasu. Her nose bleeding, she looked up at him defiantly. "I'll do it again! I'll lick every boy in your school if I'm expelled for it!"

"I won't expel you," the Principal said quietly. "Let's walk over to the horse trough and get the blood off your face."

From that day on, Zasu had a friend. At the time, she didn't know how often he had watched a little girl being ridiculed. Nor did she know, until years later, of the concern he felt when she told him about her dreams, stressing the one she longed most to become a reality—doing her "dramatic piece" on Graduation Day. But he assured her that her name would appear on the program.

It was a cool summer and not many visitors came to Santa

Cruz. The rooms in the Pitts house remained unrented, which meant that on Graduation Day Zasu would have to wear the same old rickrack dress, and not a new dotted swiss her mother had promised to make for her. Yet even this disappointment seemed unimportant as she mounted the platform in the school auditorium and hazily saw a sea of young faces surging before her.

"Please, dear God, make me say it good. Don't let me forget right in the middle."

She struck a dramatic pose, her head held high, her long thin arm sweeping a wide arc.

There was a spontaneous burst of laughter!

"Please, dear God, don't let them laugh at me."

On the second try, she dramatically thrust out both arms, her hands swinging loosely on their wrists.

Even the teachers began to laugh!

"Please, dear God . . ."

Her voice, as she started to recite, rose louder and louder so it could be heard above the other voices that threatened to drown her out. Then suddenly it broke in a thin squeak and trailed off into silence.

Stunned, she stood on the platform, her face white as a sheet. She bowed stiffly and walked off, dazed, hurt. "Dear Lord, how could you do this to me?" she asked of heaven fiercely.

"Don't stop!" the audience was calling. "Finish it. Finish it. It's the funniest thing we've ever heard!"

The Principal walked hastily to the wings and she felt his arm around her taut shoulders. "They love you, Zasu," he told her sternly. "Go back and finish it."

"They're laughing at me," she wailed.

"They're laughing *with* you. They think you're wonderful. Look here—when has the whole school ever noticed you before—wanted you for something?"

"Want me for a laugh! For a clown," she shrugged.

"What's wrong with that?" the Principal challenged. "Maybe that's your mission in life. Not many of us find our place in life, Zasu. Maybe that's what God intended. And His wisdom is greater than ours!"

Zasu took a breath. She had asked God for success—the audience was calling for her, whistling for her!

"Go on, Zasu," the Principal urged gently. "Laughter is the greatest medicine in life. It brings light into darkness. Peace to aching hearts. Riches that money could never buy."

His arm tightened around her. "Laughter," he whispered, "is God's hand upon a troubled world."

Zasu Pitts turned and walked back on stage.

She finished "The Midnight Ride of Paul Revere" to such applause as had never been heard before in the school auditorium. A coterie of little girls accompanied her home, invited her to all their parties.

"Gee, Zasu, you're funny," the boys said. There was *admiration* in their voices. "Honest, you're a scream."

Smiling, she waved one of her thin hands at them. Then as she walked up the sagging steps into her house, she repeated those words that she was always to remember, and to cherish. "Laughter is God's hand upon a troubled world."

So that's why my friend Zasu Pitts is *not* playing Lady Macbeth on Broadway today! That's why the world can count on Zasu for a laugh. The kind of laughter that is God's hand upon a troubled world.

Illustration, Zasu Pitts, see page 1

WHAT'S IN IT FOR ~~ME~~ *Him*?

by ERNIE MEHL

*Here's a meaningful discovery by the Sports Editor
of the Kansas City Star.*

SEVERAL YEARS ago I contributed an article to a series in the
Kansas City Star on: "What My Religion Means To Me."

Later the thought occurred to me that the title for the series
was inappropriate. It smacked too much of a trend which had
influenced me as I knew it had others.

What can religion mean to me? What can God mean to me?
What can the church, my job, my city, my country mean to me?
How much is there in it for me? If I do this for someone, what
can I get out of it in return?

That must have been the theory under which I lived for so
many years. If I did something, what would be my pay? I
attended churches, I sat during service and, in a sense, I defied a
minister to inspire me.

When the truth dawned on me, I realized it was not the
minister's place to inspire me any more than it was my place to
inspire the minister. It was my place to serve the church, as
much as it was the church's place to serve me. In the same way,
I could serve my job, my city, my state. My new slogan could
well be, "What's there in it for God?"

It even might be, I thought, that I could be as important to
God as God could be to me, and the more important I became
to God the more important He became to me.

My activities, my time spent, the use to which I put my money
came under new scrutiny. Under the stimulus of this line of
thinking, my life has undergone a profound change. I have

31

come to a better understanding of the seeming paradoxes which Jesus used.

And I have learned, for example, how much power you can generate when you bring God into situations involving other people.

Sometime ago two of my friends developed an extreme dislike for each other. I knew both to be fine gentlemen. But some difference, a misunderstanding or two, had been exaggerated. Now they no longer spoke.

I was fond of both these men and distressed at the situation which steadily worsened. As an intermediary I seemed to have the most dismal lack of success. One day I was pointing out to one of the men the fine qualities of the other. His face reddened. Finally he shook his finger at me.

"If you and I are to remain friends," he announced, "you will never mention his name to me again. So long as I live—and I mean this—I will never have anything to do with him."

This was said with such finality I arose from my chair beside him and walked to a water cooler. Wryly, I thought of Christ's promise, "If any man thirst, let him come unto me, and drink." *

This, I thought, is certainly one of those occasions when God could help me. It was important that these men be reconciled, and I had failed utterly so far.

So I talked with God. I told Him that I had failed. I knew nothing else to try, I asked for His help.

All this could not have consumed more than twenty or thirty seconds. When I returned to my friend's desk, he beckoned to me. "You know," he began, "maybe I am wrong. I have been wrong before. Suppose the three of us have lunch."

You could have knocked me down with a paper cup. Lunch we had, and now there is a wonderful unity and understanding amongst all three of us.

* *John 7: 37*

I have also learned that those men and women who receive the greatest spiritual benefits from life are those who contribute the most of themselves.

One of the most remarkable baseball prospects I ever saw, a young man who was potentially in a class with Joe DiMaggio or Ted Williams, made the hard decision against a baseball career.

Instead, Gus Wolff chose to remain with his aged mother and father who operated a store.

Some six or seven years ago a fall on the ice resulted in a permanent injury, and since then Gus has been confined to bed in his one-room apartment. His father and mother have since died, and he is alone.

Once a week I receive a card from Gus on which he has written: "Just to let you know I am thinking of you." Once a week or so I will get a call from him. "I have something nice to tell you and it will make you feel good," is his customary salutation.

Quite often the call comes when I am in low spirits; or when something has gone wrong. I am always cheered by it. I can understand the agony to which Gus has subjected himself in order to crawl from the bed to the telephone stand.

But he is serving others and there are many he has lifted as he has lifted me. And so he is serving God. He has not asked what life can give him, but what he can give life. How he can help God. How he can carry some of the burden for his friends.

I said to Wolff one day: "Do you enjoy doing this?" I knew his answer before he gave it to me. "I have never been happier," he said.

For me, it adds up to this: if someone does me a bad turn, I'll not cut him dead or retaliate; I'll try and love the person. If I come on a situation of need I'll try to fill the void, not escape from it. If I am troubled, I'll go to church, not just for some quiet and peace to make me feel better, but to find a job to do for God.

Illustration, Ernie Mehl, see page 1

They came up from nowhere—

PAGE 57

PAGE 53

MODERN

HORATIO

ALGER

STORIES

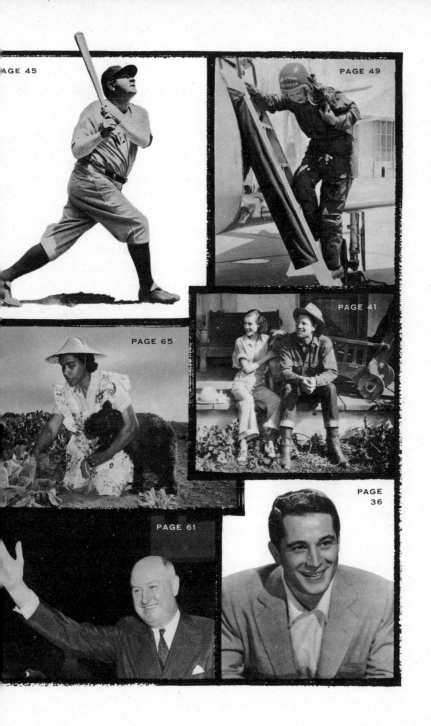

PAGE 45

PAGE 49

PAGE 65

PAGE 41

PAGE 61

PAGE 36

NO TAX ON MY HERITAGE

by **PERRY COMO**

This famous singing personality, who started as a barber, tells of a heart-warming family experience rich in the American tradition.

MY FATHER was a mill hand, and during the last 15 years of his life he was a hopeless invalid. Always vigorous and active he suddenly became sick, and could not work. It was his heart. A little group of friends would come to visit him every evening. Plain people. This is Canonsburg, Pennsylvania, a mill and mining town. These men, with the lined faces, and bent backs, and gnarled hands, who worked every day from sunup to sundown, were brought together by my father's illness. Before, they had spent their free hours in noisy play, freeing themselves from the monotonous drudgery of the mill and mine. Now, sitting there, clustered around my father, they all asked themselves: Who are we? Where do we come from?

They all had heard of God. They all believed. But they didn't work at it. They never really listened hard. Now they came within earshot of Him. There was a new light in all their faces, including my father's. It shone when he said: "Become poor in spirit and share the light with me."

At the time I didn't understand all this. I was 14. But I knew that my father was showing me how to believe in many ways. His last 15 years were years of pain, but they were the happiest years of his life.

They couldn't have been made so happy because of what he owned. Pop never made more than $175 a month. But he raised 13 kids, and not one of them a black sheep. We all worked. It was natural for me to start at the age of 11 in a barber shop.

Before school I opened the shop and lit the stoves. After school I swept the hair off the floors, polished the mirrors, and the owner taught me how to cut hair. My pay was fifty cents a week. My ambition then was to be the best barber between Canonsburg and Cleveland.

When I was 14, my father set me up in my own shop. If things got slow, I'd pick up my guitar and sing. You put someone with Italian blood down in the bleak mine country, and his only defense against the bleakness is to sing. The singing was also a reflection of the joy that came from a happy home.

By the time I was 20, I was making a big fat $40 a week. My mother and father thought that was the height of prosperity. To Pop, prosperity meant "enough to remind you to be thankful." My mother even predicted that some day I'd be making $60 a week.

Later, much later, my father never could understand what they call success in the singing business. He was always puzzled by how a man standing in front of a microphone could earn a lot of money. The first time he heard me sing was in a theatre where I was appearing. After the show I rushed to him, asking silently for his approval.

"Bravo," was all he said.

At first I was hurt. But when Pop added: "The audience . . . do all your audiences cheer you so loud and crazy?" I realized what he meant: applause every day keeps feeding your vanity and pride. And that's no way to become poor in spirit.

Besides, to people like Pop, singers meant Caruso, Martinelli, Scotti. And you know, maybe they're right.

Anyway, I wouldn't have had my father different.

And my mother, she's still teaching me how to be poor in spirit. I'd like her to come and stay with me and my wife Roselle and our three kids. But she won't. At her house in Canonsburg, with all her grandchildren, it's like a big party all the time.

She sits on the porch and everybody who comes by says hello. Up here in New York nobody says hello in quite the same way. She's probably right. To people like Mom, a little conversation with a friend is more important than running around for big things. Roselle and I and the kids get down to see her every month, and Mom still can't figure out what I do for a living. When we bring her a gift, and it's a little expensive, she looks at me suspiciously, and asks: "Where did you get the money?"

I wouldn't have her different either.

Sure, I got the things money can buy now. But the things money can't buy my mother and my father gave me.

My wife Roselle gives them to me too. She's as blonde and pretty as the day I married her 20 years ago. A year after we were married, we went off for a week's vacation to Cleveland, and there Roselle talked me into singing for a band leader named Fred Carlone.

He offered me $25 a week. That was the end of my making an honest living. But it began seven years of one-night stands, climbing on and off buses, living in flea bag hotels. Three years with Carlone, and four with another band leader named Ted Weems. Roselle traveled with me. It was like the foreign legion. We couldn't get out. No, I take that back. Going from $25 to $125 a week was a lot of money. I didn't want to get out—until our son Ronnie was on the way.

We went back home, and I was all ready to open a barber shop when I got a phone call from New York. Columbia Broadcasting offered me $76 a week on a sustaining show of my own. I hesitated. But Roselle said: "Honey, you can always open up a barber shop." I went to New York.

It was the time of the Frank Sinatra bonfire. Anyone with some hair, a set of his own teeth, and a voice that could stay in key had plenty of chances. They gave me the jackpot; theatres, night clubs, records; then they signed me to a big radio show; and I even got a movie contract. All within a few months. And now television.

It was crazy, but it was the singing business. A barber can work from 8:00 a.m. to 10:00 p.m. to make $50 a week—maybe. An engineer, a scientist, a doctor, a writer, they sweat and study long and hard before they can even start earning a buck. But in this business a guy makes one record and gets $50,000.

Somewhere along the line Someone sure put His hand on my head. I keep trying to deserve it.

We've got reason to be thankful, Roselle and I. But we never talk about it. That kind of gratitude isn't for conversation. Faith is a word for doing, not talking.

We have three kids, Ronnie is 14. We adopted two more: David, who's seven, and Terri, our daughter, who's six. We got David when he was four, and Terri when she was six months old. They all have an equal place in our hearts. They all reflect our own beliefs. But the way children believe, it's like an inner beauty that shines right through to the outside.

I see it when I know they'll all be home waiting for me to get there.

I see it when they all put their arms around me and kiss me goodnight, with the complete assurance that they're loved and wanted.

I see it when Ronnie takes the four and a half dollars he saved and asks his mother to match it so he can buy a rod and reel for his brother and take Davey fishing.

I see it every Sunday when we all march off to church together, including the maid.

And I see it shining when we sit down at the table. The kids won't start eating unless Grace is said. Who do you think says Grace? The two small ones, Davey and Terri. When they mumble, Ronnie, the sergeant, says: "Say the words so we can all understand them." And he gets them to say them over and over until they do it right.

And I see it when they say their prayers before they climb into bed every night.

I pray just like my kids do. Were my prayers ever answered? If you believe, anything you think, do, or have is an answer to prayer. If you believe, you know that without anybody having to tell it to you. Then your heart's at peace. If your heart's at peace, everything else is. If it isn't, everything else is wrong. That's the way it always is.

Everything that's ever happened to me has been the result of faith. The faith I found in my father's house, and now find in my own house, and in my world. Sure, there are different beliefs, but as long as men believe, they believe basically the same thing. The lyrics may be different, but the music is always the same.

I know now that with his illness and poverty, my Father had wealth beyond money. His heritage to his children was greater than any fortune.

That's the only heritage a man can give his children while he's alive.

It's the only one that becomes more precious after his death.

Illustration, Perry Como, see page 35

WHAT'S BEHIND LUCK?

by **JOEL McCREA**

> *"He has no 'get-up-and-go'," they said about Joel McCrea in high school. But the young actor became a big success. Was it due to luck? Read what happened when McCrea was called on the carpet by his studio boss.*

IF MY experience in motion pictures has taught me anything, it is this. No mere man is clever enough to control all the forces which must work together for all-around success in life. I do not believe in luck, nor can I take personal credit for the piloting of my own career.

While attending Hollywood High School, my fellow students said I lacked "get-up-and-go." Though ambitious, I seemed to lack drive. But my dreams were of the wide spaces, open sky and a cattle ranch.

Hollywood was a smaller town, then, and my newspaper route was star-studded. As a boy, I tossed the *Los Angeles Times* on the doorstep of Mary Pickford and Douglas Fairbanks. I was on friendly terms with others of my customers: Gloria Swanson, Wallace Reid, Cecil B. de Mille and William S. Hart.

Hart was a famous silent-screen cowboy actor. Each time I threw a paper on his porch, I imagined that my delivery bike was a horse and for a moment the paved street was a cactus-studded range.

During the summers, I worked for the King Cattle Company in the Tehachapi Mountains, where I was taught to ride the range and to farm.

To achieve my goal of a ranch, I needed capital. Acting would be a fine way to acquire this capital, I decided. It might even be fun. And the jump from a delivery bike to the silver screen isn't at all fantastic in a place like Hollywood.

My mother had some advice to offer. She had always relied on a line from the Lord's Prayer, "Thy will be done." With her, it was not a term of martyred resignation. On the contrary, it was a joyous note of confidence in a Divine harmonious plan which included all men.

If I listened for His voice, followed His guidance and wisdom instead of my own, she advised, He would lead me to my proper place. And what could I want, she asked, more than my proper place?

My father had given me 12 months in which to prove myself in pictures. Should I fail, I was to "go out and get a job." For 11 months I failed miserably, averaging 3 days a month as an extra at $7.50 a day.

One morning I awoke with a great sense of harmony, of peace, of my right relationship to the world and everyone in it. Even the rain outside, which would make moist hunting of my daily studio rounds, seemed a blessing. I could wear my new trench coat, a prized possession.

I was standing outside the door of the RKO casting office when a producer went by. A mighty man with parts to give, he looked me over carefully. My heart rose. He passed into his office without a word. My heart sank. But in a minute he was back, "You," he called. "Come in here."

I stood in his office, a little damp, but feeling again that sense of rightness. "This," thought I, "is it."

"What do you do around here?" he asked.

"I'm an actor," I said, stretching the truth a bit.

"Where did you get that trench coat?"

I couldn't believe my ears. "Place up in Hollywood," I faltered.

"How much?"

"Eighteen dollars."

"I like it," he said. "Could you get me one?" I watched him peel off a twenty and then I was out in the rain again, trudging three miles because I didn't want to waste carfare. And he didn't even tip me.

Next morning our phone rang. It was the producer. "Are you the trench coat fellow?" he demanded. "I've been thinking about you," he said. "Didn't you say you were an actor? We just bought a story, and the guy in it. . . . Well, you *are* the guy. Built the same. Look the same. You better come back here."

There it was. The open door. Luck? Maybe. Maybe once . . . or twice. But when you find you can apply a certain principle to every phase of life, at any given moment, it can't be just luck. Through the years I have followed the principle of "asking my way of Him," and then confidently taking the next step which seems right.

Several years ago, for example, a major studio had a call on me for one picture a year. That is a commitment and, in the last analysis, I could be forced to do that picture whether I liked the part or not.

One day I was mailed a script which had me playing the lead opposite one of our foremost glamour girls. My agent was delighted. "She's never made a picture that's lost money. She's great box office."

But I didn't like the story, nor my part. It was a distasteful, degrading one, I thought. Nor did I personally care for the torrid story any more than I could see myself as the lover.

Starting with the producer, I carefully explained why I did not want to make the picture. He referred me to the executive producer, who passed me on to the executive, executive producer. Each time I repeated my explanation until my own monologue was beginning to bore me. And all it got me was a date to explain my feelings to the big boss.

I valued my reputation for co-operation. Never had I been forced to be "difficult," to refuse a part. I didn't want to now. And a contract is a contract. Nevertheless, I felt strongly I shouldn't do this picture. It was, you might say, a dilemma. And as I faced the chief executive, a man reputed to be ruthless and deaf to any pleas, I knew that beyond this office I had no further recourse.

He looked at me with cold eyes and said abruptly, "I don't want a long story. I want just one *good* reason why you don't want to play this part."

In a moment of silence, I reached mentally for help. Then I said slowly, "I would be embarrassed to have my sons see me in this picture."

For a second he just stared. Then he stood up, clapped me on the shoulder and said, "I see you have given this honest thought. . . . Maybe you'd like to do a Western we're working on?"

Was that a "lucky" line? I don't think so. Was I clever? I know I wasn't. It was truth speaking in me, recognized by the producer, and harmony between us was the inevitable result.

I don't claim I haven't made mistakes. I have. But most of my mistakes were due to trusting "luck," or my own judgment instead of His.

Illustration, Joel McCrea and wife, Frances Dee, see page 35

THE KIDS CAN'T TAKE IT IF WE DON'T GIVE IT

by GEORGE HERMAN "BABE" RUTH

In the last weeks before his death, Babe Ruth gave
Guideposts *his most important message*

BAD BOY RUTH—that was me.

Don't get the idea that I'm proud of my harum-scarum youth. I'm not. I simply had a rotten start in life, and it took me a long time to get my bearings.

Looking back to my youth, I honestly don't think I knew the difference between right and wrong. I spent much of my early boyhood living over my father's saloon, in Baltimore—and when I wasn't living over it, I was in it, soaking up the atmosphere. I hardly knew my parents.

St. Mary's Industrial School in Baltimore, where I was finally taken, has been called an orphanage and a reform school. It was, in fact, a training school for orphans, incorrigibles, delinquents, and runaways picked up on the streets of the city. I was listed as an incorrigible. I guess I was. Perhaps I would always have been but for Brother Matthias, the greatest man I have ever known, and for the religious training I received there which has since been so important to me.

I doubt if any appeal could have straightened me out except a Power over and above man—the appeal of God. Iron-rod discipline couldn't have done it. Nor all the punishment and reward systems that could have been devised. God had an eye out for me, just as He has for you, and He was pulling for me to make the grade.

As I look back now, I realize that knowledge of God was a big crossroads with me. I got one thing straight (and I wish all kids did)—that God was Boss. He was not only my Boss but Boss of all my bosses. Up till then, like all bad kids, I hated most of the people who had control over me and could punish me. I began to see that I had a higher Person to reckon with who never changed, whereas my earthly authorities changed from year to year. Those who bossed me had the same self-battles—they, like me, had to account to God. I also realized that God was not only just, but merciful. He knew we were weak and that we all found it easier to be stinkers than good sons of God, not only as kids but all through our lives.

That clear picture, I'm sure, would be important to any kid who hates a teacher, or resents a person in charge. This picture of my relationship to man and God was what helped relieve me of bitterness and rancor and a desire to get even.

I've seen a great number of "he-men" in my baseball career, but never one equal to Brother Matthias. He stood six feet six and weighed 250 pounds. It was all muscle. He could have been successful at anything he wanted to in life—and he chose the church.

It was he who introduced me to baseball. Very early he noticed that I had some natural talent for throwing and catching. He used to back me in a corner of the big yard at St. Mary's and bunt a ball to me by the hour, correcting the mistakes I made with my hands and feet. I never forgot the first time I saw him hit a ball. The baseball in 1902 was a lump of mush, but Brother Matthias would stand at the end of the yard, throw the ball up with his left hand, and give it a terrific belt with the bat he held in his right hand. The ball would carry 350 feet, a tremendous knock in those days. I would watch him bugeyed.

Thanks to Brother Matthias I was able to leave St. Mary's in 1914 and begin my professional career with the famous Baltimore Orioles. Out on my own ... free from the rigid rules of a religious school ... boy, did it go to my head. I began really to cut capers.

I strayed from the church, but don't think I forgot my religious training. I just overlooked it. I prayed often and hard, but, like many irrepressible young fellows, the swift tempo of my living shoved religion into the background.

So what good was all the hard work and ceaseless interest of the Brothers, people would argue? You can't make kids religious, they say, because it just won't take. Send kids to Sunday School and they too often end up hating it and the Church.

Don't you believe it. As far as I'm concerned, and I think as far as most kids go, once religion sinks in, it stays there—deep down. The lads who get religious training, get it where it counts—in the roots. They may fail it, but it never fails them. When the score is against them, or they get a bum pitch, that unfailing Something inside will be there to draw on.

I've seen it with kids. I know from the letters they write me.

The more I think of it, the more important I feel it is to give kids "the works" as far as religion is concerned. They'll never want to be holy—they'll act like tough monkeys in contrast, but somewhere inside will be a solid little chapel. It may get dusty from neglect, but the time will come when the door will be opened with much relief. But the kids can't take it, if we don't give it to them.

I've been criticized as often as I'm praised for my activities with kids on the grounds that what I did was for publicity. Well, criticism doesn't matter. I never forgot where I came from. Every dirty-faced kid I see is another useful citizen. No one knew better than I what it meant not to have your own home, a backyard, and your own kitchen and ice box. That's why all through the years, even when the big money was rolling in, I'd never forget St. Mary's, Brother Matthias, and the boys I left behind. I kept going back.

As I look back those moments when I let the kids down—they were my worst. I guess I was so anxious to enjoy life to the fullest that I forgot the rules—or ignored them. Once in a while you can get away with it, but not for long. When I broke training, the effects were felt by myself and by the ball team—and even by the fans.

While I drifted away from the Church, I did have my own "altar," a big window of my New York apartment overlooking the city lights. Often I would kneel before that window and say my prayers. I would feel quite humble then. I'd ask God to help me not make such a big fool of myself and pray that I'd measure up to what He expected of me.

In December 1946 I was in French Hospital, New York, facing a serious operation. Paul Carey, one of my oldest and closest friends, was by my bed one night.

"They're going to operate in the morning, Babe," Paul said. "Don't you think you ought to put your house in order?"

I didn't dodge the long, challenging look in his eyes. I knew what he meant. For the first time I realized that death might strike me out. I nodded, and Paul got up, called in a chaplain, and I made a full confession.

"I'll return in the morning and give you Holy Communion," the chaplain said, "but you don't have to fast."

"I'll fast," I said. I didn't have even a drop of water.

As I lay in bed that evening I thought to myself what a comforting feeling to be free from fear and worries. I now could simply turn them over to God. Later on, my wife brought in a letter from a little kid in Jersey City.

"Dear Babe," he wrote. "Everybody in the seventh-grade class is pulling and praying for you. I am enclosing a medal which if you wear will make you better. Your pal—Mike Quinlan.

P.S. I know this will be your 61st homer. You'll hit it."

I asked them to pin the Miraculous Medal to my pajama coat. I've worn the medal constantly ever since. I'll wear it to my grave.

Illustration, Babe Ruth, see page 35

HOW TO FIND ADVENTURE

by JACQUELINE COCHRAN

Here is the fabulous story of an orphan who quit school at 9 to work the all night shift in a cotton mill. One adventure followed another. Learning to fly, she lived through 12 crashes and was the first woman to fly a jet faster than sound! But that's just a small sample of the accomplishments of this amazing girl who lives by God's exciting promise ... "Seek, and ye shall find".

WHATEVER adventures or accomplishments are mine the past twenty years would hardly have been possible without an important truth I stumbled on as a child: God can give an ordinary person the power to achieve extraordinary things. I know that in every fibre of my being. Consider my beginnings:

I do not know when I was born, nor who my parents were.

As far as memory serves, I started life as a sort of waif or unadopted orphan in a shack in a Florida sawmill camp. It was Sawdust Road, pretty much like Tobacco Road. My bed was a pallet on the floor.

My foster father worked as a mill hand—when work was available. During these fortunate periods we had the luxury of sowbelly and beans, plus any fish I could catch. Between jobs it was mostly fish. Even before I knew the stork was a bird, I helped deliver babies for the women in camp who could not afford a midwife or doctor. The few odd pennies I acquired this way bought me my first toothbrush.

I had one year of schooling, and hung around my teacher's house before and after school, hungry for more knowledge about the world. When she told me of places up north where there

With credit to "The Stars At Noon" by Jacqueline Cochran (Little, Brown & Co.)

was more than sowbelly and beans, my imagination was airborne.

At the age of eight, I tried to join a band of gypsies, but they would have no part of me. Then I attempted to join a little circus, but fell asleep while it broke camp and was left behind.

Somehow I pushed my way north, and many nights during that long journey I would look up at the stars and the moon. How I wanted to be up there traveling as fast as they were! And looking at them I also knew I was not alone.

In Columbus, Georgia, I got a job, working the twelve-hour night shift in a cotton mill. I was nine by then. The wages were seven cents an hour. With my own money I bought my first pair of shoes.

Even in retrospect about these days I am thankful because God has taught me that I can never have so little that I haven't had less.

There was a strike in the cotton mill that lasted a long time. When I got hungry, the forelady of the mill helped me get a job as a roustabout in a beauty parlor.

During this time I had my first view of an airport. My heart soared when I saw my first plane. I knew then how I could travel with the stars.

But the determination to fly did not come until years later. I was working in New York for Antoine's, the beauty shop in Saks Fifth Avenue, when they sent me to Miami to represent them for the winter season. At a dinner party my partner was Floyd B. Odlum. It was the first time we had met, and I told him of my dreams and hopes, and the immediate aim of selling cosmetics on the road, and starting my own company.

"To do that job well, you should learn to fly," he said.

"I will," I replied very quickly, and I knew I soon would.

Three weeks later I was back in New York and asked for a brief vacation. The next day I was taking a free demonstration flight. After three hours of instruction, I soloed. And on my first flight the engine quit on me! I made it back to the field on dead stick, praying all the way. In 17 days I had my private flying license.

In time, my flying served as a passport through many doors. It took me into the palaces of kings and queens, shahs, and other rulers, and to a private audience with the Pope. Whenever I was among them, I could always see the little girl buying her first pair of shoes with her wages from the cotton mill.

I have found that it is as easy to reach for the moon as it is to reach for the top of the fence that hems you in—if one mixes ambition and imagination. Of course, the mixture must contain a base of honesty, and the whole must be blended with faith.

Perhaps faith was inherent in my case. It was partly developed through the help of a traveling priest who visited our sawmill camp on occasion. I was a child then, but I sensed the light of God in this priest, and it shone on me. Even a child can thrill to the promise: "Ask, and it shall be given you; seek, and ye shall find; knock, and it shall be opened unto you."*

Because I have a strong faith and believe in prayer, does not mean that everything always comes out right for me. There have been turbulence and air pockets. In the early days of my more than 10,000 hours of flying, I must have had a hundred forced landings and a dozen crack-ups, but I walked away from all of them.

My first place of business was destroyed by a hurricane. Four of my planes were also destroyed. Once, while flying just 200 feet above the ground at close to 700 miles an hour, I set a new speed record only to find on landing that the electrical timing equipment on the ground had not functioned and my efforts had gone for naught.

Recently, I became the first woman to pass the sonic barrier

* *Matthew 7: 7*

and to exceed the speed of sound. That meant a climb to an altitude of nearly 50,000 feet. Up there, even by day, the sky is dark blue, and the stars can be seen. Earthbound friends are left behind.

But up there I did not feel alone. Indeed, I felt closer to the portals of Heaven, and more aware of the presence of God. When your innermost self is being tested, there is no dependence on the material world below. You cannot see or hear those dear to you. But you find yourself in Hands more gentle and trustworthy than human hands can ever be. Their invisible influence filled my being, and I was fortified for the moment when I turned the nose of my plane down into a full power dive.

Those Hands never left me during the subsequent antics of the plane and fighting the turbulent shock waves of the barrier. The speed I attained was well in excess of 700 miles an hour.

Flying through the sound barrier is like flying inside an explosion. In the dive the plane creates a shock wave, and when it pulls out of the dive the shock wave speeds straight down toward earth, and strikes the earth with two whip-crack explosions. In my first dive these explosions were heard on the flight line, but were not recorded in the observation tower. I was heartsick. That same day, however, I went back up again and repeated the dive so they could be recorded properly. Two weeks later I did it again.

I have found adventure in flying, in world travel, in business and even close at hand. There can be adventure in such a simple pastime as my helping the wild quail on our ranch lose their fear and come trustfully close to me.

Adventure is a state of mind—and spirit. It comes through faith—for with complete faith there is no fear of what faces one in life or death.

Illustration, Jacqueline Cochran, see page 35

I DIDN'T GET AWAY WITH IT

by **ROY ROGERS**

This cowboy star once had to shoot rabbits to live. He also drove a gravel truck, picked peaches, worked on a construction crew, and played the guitar on the side. He learned to handle all situations well—except one.

WHAT'S WRONG with a guy who isn't scared when he nearly breaks his neck filming Western pictures, but gets the shakes when he has to make a simple speech? For years I asked myself this question.

I was shy from my boyhood days when we lived on the Ohio River in a three-room houseboat built by my father. Our family—Mother, Dad, and three sisters—later settled on a farm outside Portsmouth, Ohio. Dad worked in a shoe factory, while my sisters and I helped Mother run the farm.

By the time I was ten I could call a square dance and play the guitar. But to get up and talk before a class, or just a few people, would make me take off across the cornfields.

I earned a dollar a week by ploughing corn on neighborhood farms, later quit school and went to work in the shoe factory to help out the family finances. When the family went to visit my sister in California, I fell in love with the far West.

I drove a gravel truck in Lawndale, California for a while, then during the depression took any kind of job. I helped build a state highway from Newhall to Castaic, later joined the "Okies," and picked peaches in the California fruit orchards described in "The Grapes of Wrath."

During my spare time I practiced on my guitar, hoping that some day I could make a living as a musician and a singer. Three of us formed a musical trio called the Texas Outlaws, but it was rough going. In our travels we often had to go out and shoot rabbits to live.

Then, as often happens to a guy who wanders into Hollywood, I had a lucky break, got a spot in a picture and my film career started. When my wife died during the birth of our third child, I was faced with a demanding career and the responsibilities of raising three fine children.

The story I want to tell begins several years later. Dale Evans, a film star in her own right, and I had been making pictures together for many years. With the unanimous approval of my children, we were married on December 31, 1948.

We hadn't been married but a few days when she started one morning with "It's a beautiful day to go to church!"

Now I wasn't a stranger to churches. I just hadn't time to get acquainted with very many because of other things I preferred doing. "Honey, I've gotta go see Joe Miller this morning," I said quickly. "Why don't you go ahead without me?"

This was the first excuse I could think of, but with more advance warning I could have done much better. Dale fixed a firm eye on me, and I knew her nimble mind was working overtime. She let me get away with it the first time, but going to church soon became the most important thing to do on Sunday.

One night before going to bed I noticed a new book on my reading table. "Where did this come from?" I asked, picking up a copy of the Bible.

"Since you lost your old one, I bought it for you this morning," Dale said brightly. She knew that I knew I never had a copy of the Bible, but what can you do with a woman whose mind is made up!

Grace before meals became a regular thing. Cheryl, Linda and Roy, Jr., (the three children of my first marriage) were quick to take a part. Dale introduced a type of Grace where everyone said a sentence prayer.

I would squirm in my chair a little, hoping they wouldn't notice me. So it went around the table, then "Why don't you say something, Daddy?" Linda piped up.

Dale, God bless her, is the smartest and most loving woman in the world. She didn't press me; but she never lets go of an idea she thinks is right.

Later, when I tried to explain my feelings to Dale, she would say, "The Lord gave you many talents, Roy. Some you use well for yourself, but there are some you haven't developed at all for Him. If you could learn to let God speak through you, honey, you could make a good speech every time—and not die doing it."

I didn't know what she meant at first. To some people, religion may come in one big emotional experience. I moved to it a step at a time: regular attendance at church, reading a few passages from the Bible, saying Grace. A warm quality grew into our family life. It was a spiritual kind of love that makes you want to do something for others.

A group of people in Hollywood began to get together and talk about all these things, people like Tim Spencer, Red Harper, Colleen Townsend, Jane Russell, Mrs. Henrietta Meers, Connie Haines, Joyce Compton, Dale, myself and others. We would meet at different homes, some of us bringing along extra chairs. There was prayer for the problems of others; several would speak of religion out of their own experience.

I never had enough education to understand theology, but when a fellow like Tim Spencer stands up before a group like this and tells frankly how his belief in Jesus Christ helped him change from a drunk to a hard-working citizen, then Christianity comes alive to me.

One day I discovered that I actually looked forward to saying the blessing at mealtime. It may sound corny, but I could hardly wait for my turn. I began to appreciate the wholesome things that happen in each area of life when you're right with God. Not that I don't have plenty far to go.

The biggest triumph came when I used Dale's suggestion about speaking in public. The occasion was like many others. The music part I handled without any fear, but when it came time to say a few words, I felt the same old nervous symptoms. Then I closed my eyes for just a moment and said silently, "Lord, I'll just make a mess of things on my own. Help me to relax a little so that what I say will really mean something."

I started to talk and found myself saying things I'd never said before. And they came out as naturally as though I was just standing there and someone else was talking. From that time, I've never had more than the normal amount of nervousness.

Our faith was tested less than two years ago with the death of our 2-year-old daughter, Robin Elizabeth. Although physically handicapped from birth, Robin touched ours and other lives deeply, and I questioned why one so young had to suffer.

Yet out of this tragedy came Dale's book about Robin, "Angel Unaware," which she started in anguish and finished with a deep sense of understanding and a feeling that Robin's mission was truly being accomplished. Nearly 300,000 copies have been sold, proceeds of the book going to the National Association for Retarded Children. Robin Elizabeth, in two years, made her life count more than some of us do in a lifetime.

Illustration, Roy Rogers and "Trigger," see page 34

HOW TO LOVE YOUR WAY
OUT OF THE KITCHEN

by **HELEN FERGUSON**

*As a young girl she dreamed of success as an actress
—but all she could find was a job washing dishes.
"Why aren't my prayers answered?" she com-
plained. Then a friend gave Helen Ferguson a wonderful formula for self pity.*

WHEN I arrived in New York at the age of sixteen, I had $28.00
in my purse and a scrapbook of clippings which chronicled my
budding career as a motion picture actress in Chicago.

But my real equipment for success lay in my complete faith in
the power of prayer; in my gratitude that I was an American.
In America, my mother had taught me, one could earn anything
one was willing to work hard for.

Within six weeks my money was spent, I was homesick, my
shoes needed resoling, and I was stranded in a brownstone front
rooming-house in Brooklyn.

But I wasn't scared. You can't be scared when your heart is
filled with faith, your mind filled with prayer.

I had to have a roof over my head, so I made a deal with my
landlady. She moved me into a dinky attic room, and for that
heatless cubicle I agreed to do the daily clean-up work on all four
floors.

I soon discovered my deep, stark hatred of the ugly kitchen.
Despite my most energetic attentions, it always looked dreary.
And I hated washing dishes. Passionately, I hated that endless,
unrewarding task.

I was also filled with self-pity. A leading lady in Chicago, here
I was washing dishes in an ugly house in Brooklyn, making no
money to send home to my mother and sister.

I was furious with resentment. I hated, even, every cup and

saucer. I had to pay for each cup, saucer, plate or glass I broke. And I broke more each day.

It was hard to pray through all that hate and self-pity.

Sunday School was an oasis in my misery and bewilderment. It was like holding my mother's hand. And finally, what a blessing came from confiding my problem to my Sunday School teacher.

"I just don't understand," I said flatly. "Why aren't my prayers answered?"

"Because you 'pray amiss,' Helen," she said gently. "You have been taught that Divine Love alone governs man, protects and directs him; that hatred never solved a problem nor dissolved an obstacle. Love, though, will do both."

"You mean I have to love that kitchen?"

"You don't have to love that kitchen, but you do have to love your way out of it. Unless, of course, you're happy hating it."

That loving rebuke brought the humble realization that I had been dictating to God, thereby not following my religious training at all.

It was a tall order, I thought, as I walked "home." But it had to be filled. I started being grateful that I had a place to live. And from that small gratefulness, the expense of replacing broken dishes stopped. Because—I stopped breaking them!

I found myself taking a pride in the *cleanness* of the kitchen. Then, in the neatness of its shelves. I bought some bright paper and was delighted at the *happy* look of those shelves. Under this enthusiasm I spent a hard-earned dollar on bright calico, and then I persuaded the landlady to make perkily ruffled curtains. I coaxed a discouraged geranium bud to grow into an ambitious red bloom in a pot around which I'd wrapped a bit of crisp crepe paper.

And I was so proud and happy with my production!

I don't know, nor can I ever remember, just when hate left. Suddenly all was lovely, and hate was gone. The landlady never thanked me, but one night I discovered a new pillow case on my bed. At the store one day I learned she'd invited the neighbors in to view the kitchen and had said, "The child will go where she wants. Work don't scare that one."

In a burst of gratitude I rushed to the dime store and bought a half-dozen sparkling glasses as a gift for *my* kitchen. When I reached it there was a message. My first call from the Edward Small Agency!

My work was done in that house. I had literally and spiritually loved my way out of it. I had gained a positive, scientific rule for overcoming anything that could overwhelm me.

There is really no end to my kitchen story. Its principle is ever-present in my business and social life, and proving that principle—over and over—is one of life's continuing adventures. I wish I could say I always prove it instantly and unfailingly. I would feel far more deserving if I could say that.

The warfare with oneself is not fought in a sparkling arena, but in some murky corner of consciousness which, when one has loved enough, becomes bright and gay and peaceful because love glows there.

My picture career climbed steadily, carrying me from New York to Hollywood. The things I dreamed of doing came into existence whenever I demonstrated the scientific power of prayer.

When my first husband passed away, I retired permanently from the screen, and two years later married again. In 1932, at the nadir of a depression, my husband's bank closed; he was completely broken in the crash.

Could I now, with four step-children to support, resist resentment, disappointment and fear of the future and rely unquestioningly on Divine Love to meet my every human need?

I wasn't sixteen this time—and I *was* scared. Until I took stock on a comparative basis. I wasn't sixteen, but I was wiser. And most important of all, I had the proved and tested equipment for success: faith in prayer, gratitude that I was an American, and I still believed what Mother had taught me—one could earn anything one was willing to work hard for.

In 1933, in the fogs of depression, with no one, humanly, to back me, I started in business: Helen Ferguson, Publicity.

During my years as an actress I had always felt there was a need to raise the accepted level of Hollywood publicity—a need to picture most of its citizenry accurately.

I called or wrote dozens of prospective clients. I heard from none of them. I sat in my tiny $15-a-month office and waited. Nobody came. It could have been like my first weeks in my land-lady's kitchen so long ago except . . . this time I already knew the principle to be proved. If I was about my Father's business, doing whatever was at hand with love, my human needs would be met.

Ten days later lovely Fay Wray became my first client. Three months later I moved to a larger office, and four months after that had my own building with four offices. My husband passed on 11 years ago. I have eight offices today; clients who are also my friends; my step-children are all grown and married. Mother and I share a spacious home.

It *is* a success story. I know that. I am humbly grateful for my participation in it, but it is not a *personal* success story. It is the story of the success of a principle, a principle available to all.

Every day I remember the words of my Sunday School teacher, "Never for an instant stop loving—for in that instant you deny your identification with Him—reject His power to help you. Never circumscribe God by outlining what action He shall take. Take your own actions carefully, fearlessly, lovingly, trust God to bring about the right result."

When, as too often happens, anything less is recorded in my experience, it is because I have, for that space of time, failed in my obedience—forgotten, if ever so briefly, the story of my kitchen.

Illustration, Helen Ferguson, see page 34

BOYS WILL BE BIG SHOTS

by **JAMES A. FARLEY**

Why do boys become criminals? Whose responsibility is it? A challenge to everyone by one of America's most distinguished political figures.

WHEN I LOOK on the older generation, *my* generation, struggling with terrifying world conditions, I realize the wonders we have achieved, the advances we have made, the marked improvements and progress. Yet I also see the errors we committed, the mistakes, the wrongs, the many, many stupidities, and my heart is heavy.

When I look upon the generation after us, which was so often called "The Lost Generation," I marvel at their magnificence in World War II and in Korea. They were boys to make the blood sing and the heart exult with pride. Those were our G.I.'s who are now pulling the load with us.

But most important is the *new* young lot. Everywhere I meet them—they are the American leaders and lawmakers of tomorrow. I am deeply impressed as I talk with them by their sincerity, their directness and their capacity for devotion. These are the men of tomorrow—the bosses and law-makers. These are the men who will be and are making the United States.

Yet you and I know that the majority of our criminals are boys and young men. The average age of men who are inmates in prisons and reformatories is under 26.

American youngsters are no fools. They don't follow the hypocrite or the lukewarm. They are furnaces of strength, fierce interests, and urgent dreams. They want to be recognized. They want credit. They crave to stand out. They want desperately to be a part of doings.

What are we doing for them and about them? The problem is

not juvenile delinquency, but adult indifference. The time to stop delinquency is before the boy becomes delinquent ... at an age when most adults consider them too much bother.

The farther I go in years, the boy I was draws closer to me. With each passing birthday I see more of what I am in what I was.

I was born at Grassy Point, New York, of second generation Irish stock, the second of five boys, my brothers being John, Phil, Tom, and Bill. My schooling began at five years of age, and included High School and a year's course in a commercial school.

The things we boys took for granted in a small town would be privileges beyond purchase to our city lads. We had open fields, hills, streams, trees, animals, birds, fenceless spaces. We had fishing and swimming and plenty of space to mark out a baseball lot. We had coasting, skating and the big popcorn or candy-making feasts around outdoor fires.

We had the blessing of needed work. You can't live in the country without going miles to school or market, without tending furnaces, clearing walks, caring for chickens, horses or cows or other stock, and knowing a garden with your knees.

My father was killed by a horse when I was ten. Mother was left a small insurance policy and a half interest in a little schooner that carried brick 30 miles down the Hudson to the big city.

Maybe we five sons didn't feel *responsible!* And therefore *important.* I ran errands and did chores until mother bought a small business with her last $1,000. Then we really had responsibility. During the summer I also worked from 3:30 to 11:00 A.M. as a machine boy in Morrissy's brickyard for less than a dollar a day.

Hardship? No, it was a prideful achievement to a boy with the stirrings of manhood in him to be pulling his weight and to be needed. I still found time to be the local waltzing champion, and at eight I was carrying a torch in a "Bryan-for-President" parade, and I never missed church. I took a confirmation vow never to drink or smoke, and I've kept it.

Perhaps the two greatest blessings I had in boyhood were a fierce love of my parents and a deep devotion to my religion. These are woven in the fabric of the man that boy was. On every election day my whole life through I've gone to the graves of my mother and father and prayed.

A few years ago I saw an inter-church world survey of statistics in cities of over 300,000 population, 52.7 per cent of which were non-church going people. In rural areas the percentage was even higher. What has happened to us?

Speaking as a father and a churchman, I ask you, what can we expect of our boys when more than half of our homes are religious jungles? It is not going to be easy in the years ahead to keep and to build our democratic way of life. Are we to expect the men who take our places to do it without God? Only a vast religious awakening can give full value and unassailable dignity to our lives.

Every boy needs a leader. One reason so many become criminals is because they follow the wrong leaders. A boy has far more idealism than some people suspect. He will work. He will take rules and follow them—and even keep in strict training. He will struggle to qualify at great personal sacrifice. If he is convinced, no fooling, there is a job to be done, he will *give*.

Anybody can collect a gang of boys and throw a basketball up in the air. But when you build on a church you give a boy identification with the power of God Almighty. When you take him into a club or a purposeful group you build stability and the sense of *belonging*.

No doubt your church has a Cub pack and your Legion Post has a troop. Maybe it takes care of 20, 30, 60 boys. We also have, thank God, Boy Scouts, Big Brothers and other great organizations. But do *you* see to it that there's room for every boy in the neighborhood? Groups for the fellows too old to join a youngster group? And a pack for the little chaps in their most tender and impressionable years?

Beyond games and entertainment, skills and crafts, there must be projects to achieve at every age level. Goal after goal can be set up and won. Tomorrow's men must feel the elation of tough, worthwhile constructive *doing* . . . some eyesore cleaned, some foul spot in the community righted, some needed job done, some vital equipment earned, or a structure built. In being part and parcel of the community he helped to better, the boy will give a piece of his raw love to that spot and the people in it.

Every man can take on one boy, even form a group of 5 or 10 boys. Nightly they roam the streets and lanes longing for companionship and acceptance. Many are from broken homes. Many never heard of God. Many see their elders living and dying without God or with just enough of the church to get married and buried in.

Each of us can teach at least one boy the glory of God and the excitement of doing. Lots of people overlook that joy completely in the idea that if a man is smart enough he can find ways to live without working. Maybe an individual can, for a while, but a nation, never. The trend has become to do as little as we can and get as much as we can. Perhaps that is a far-swing of a pendulum. And it had better swing back before our red-blooded boys sicken and rot.

But there's a right way and a wrong way. Without respect for God there can be no respect for each other, past animal urges. There's a God to be honored and served because His Spirit is in us and our own spirit claims honor and service.

Tomorrow's manhood is at your elbow. Can you put out your hand and take hold of him? He's knocking at the door that is *your* future. Will you open it to him? With God in your heart and in your welcome? No man or woman, aware of our dangers today, should be able to sleep soundly without giving some share of time to our future men, individually and collectively.

Illustration, James Farley, see page 35

MY MOTHER'S GIFT—
GRACE BEFORE GREATNESS

Toscanini once said, "A voice like Marian Ander-
son's is heard only once in a hundred years." It al-
most was never heard at all...

FAILURE and frustration are in the unwritten pages of everyone's record. I have had my share of them. But if my mother's
gentle hands were not there to guide me, perhaps my life in
music would have ended long ago.

The faith my mother taught me is my foundation. It is the
only ground on which I stand. With it I have a freedom in life
I could not have in any other way. Whatever is in my voice,
my faith has put it there.

Her presence runs through everything I ever wanted to be.
The particular religion a child echoes is an accident of birth.
But I was converted to my mother's faith and patient under-
standing long before I could define either.

We were poor folk. But there was a wealth in our poverty, a
wealth of music, and love and faith. My two sisters, Alice and
Ethel, and I were all in the church choir—the junior, not the
senior one. There is still a vivid memory of our mother and
father, their faces shining with pride, watching us from the front
pews. And when I was six I was once fortunate enough to be
selected to step out in front of the choir and sing "The Lord Is
My Shepherd."

It was a Baptist Church we attended in Philadelphia. But my
mother taught us early that the form of one's faith is less important than what's in one's heart.

"When you come to Him," she said, "He never asks what you
are."

We children never heard her complain about her lot; or criticize those who offended her. One of her guiding precepts has always been: "Never abuse those who abuse you. Bear them no malice, and theirs will disappear."

My sisters still attend the Baptist Church in Philadelphia. It is a church and a congregation I hold most fondly in my heart for many reasons. These were the people who, years ago, pooled their pennies into what they grandly called "The Fund for Marian Anderson's Future," a gesture of love and confidence impossible to forget in a lifetime. When I come to Philadelphia, I always try to see some of these people who have been so important to me, and though it seldom is possible these days, I love to sing in their choir.

My father died when I was twelve, and my mother's burden became heavier. Before she became a housewife, and the mother of three daughters, she was a schoolteacher. Now she became a father to us as well as a mother and earned our whole livelihood by taking in washing. It was terribly difficult for her, I know, but she would not even hear of any of us children leaving school for work.

During these years I began to have my first opportunity to earn a little money by singing. Almost entirely they were Sunday evening concerts for the church, or for the YWCA and the YMCA. At these affairs I could sing, perhaps, two or three songs, and my fee was a very grand 50 cents, or once in a great while, $1.00. Sometimes I would dash to four or five of these concerts in one evening.

Many people were kind to me: teachers who took no fees, those who urged me forward when I was discouraged. Gradually I began to sing with glee clubs and churches in other cities. After one minor effort in Harlem, a group of well-meaning people hastily sponsored me for a concert in Town Hall in New York.

It seemed at once incredible and wonderful. But I wasn't ready: indeed, I was far from it either in experience or maturity. On the exciting night of my first real concert I was told Town Hall was sold out. While waiting in dazed delight to go on, my sponsor said there would be a slight delay. I waited five, ten, fifteen minutes. Then peeked through the curtain.

The house was half empty! I died inside. But when the curtain went up I sang my heart out. And when the concert was over, I knew I had failed. The critics next day agreed with me, but what they said was really not so important. I was shattered because within me I felt I had let down all those people who had faith and confidence in me. It seemed irrevocable.

"I'd better forget all about singing, and do something else," I told my mother.

"Why don't you think about it a little, and pray a lot, first?" she cautioned.

She had taught me to make my own decisions when I could, and pray for the right ones when I could not. But I did not heed her now. I refused a few offers to sing at other concerts. I avoided my music teacher. For a whole year I brooded in silence. My mother suffered because I was not expressing myself in the only way I knew happiness. But she knew I had to find my own way back alone. From time to time she just prodded me, gently:

"Have you prayed, Marian? Have you prayed?"

No, I hadn't. Nothing would help. I embraced my grief. It was sufficient. But in those tearful hours there slowly came the thought that there is a time when even the most self-sufficient cannot find enough strength to stand alone. Then, one prays with a fervor one never had before. From my torment I prayed with the sure knowledge there was Someone to Whom I could pour out the greatest need of my heart and soul. It did not matter if He answered. It was enough to pray.

Slowly I came out of my despair. My mind began to clear.

No one was to blame for my failure. Self pity left me. In a burst of exuberance I told my mother:

"I want to study again. I want to be the best, and be loved by everyone, and be perfect in everything."

"That's a wonderful goal," she chided. "But our dear Lord walked this earth as the most perfect of all beings, yet not everybody loved Him."

Subdued, I decided to return to my music to seek humbleness before perfection.

One day I came home from my teacher unaware that I was humming. It was the first music I had uttered at home in a whole year. My mother heard it, and she rushed to meet me, and put her arms around me and kissed me. It was her way of saying:

"Your prayers have been answered, and mine have too."

For a brief moment we stood there silently. Then my mother defined the sweet spell of our gratitude:

"Prayer begins where human capacity ends," she said.

The golden echo of that moment has always been with me through the years of struggle that followed. Today I am blessed with an active career, and the worldly goods that come with it. If sometimes I do not hear the echo and listen only to the applause, my mother reminds me quickly of what should come first:

"Grace must always come before greatness," she says.

Illustration, Marian Anderson, see page 35

WHO OWNS THE LAND?

by STARR WEST JONES

> *An immigrant boy came to America with 35 dollars and one consuming dream—to own his own farm. How he achieved his goal, step by step, is told here by his neighbor (and Guideposts Associate Editor) Starr Jones.*

WITH BIG, knuckled hands, Arnulf Muller buttoned his mackinaw collar and turned a kindly, weathered face to the Farmingdale agricultural students who had spent the day tramping over his 380 acre dairy farm. Arnulf was successful; he was what they hoped to be. Now he tried hard to give clear-cut answers to their questions.

"Just how much money does it take to start in farming today?" said one young man.

"It isn't how much money you have," said Muller, "or what your father was, or even where you went to school. It's doing right with the land that counts. Your reputation and experience are worth more than any dollars and cents you may ever have in the bank."

"Just what is the right thing?"

"And how can you own a farm without dollars, first, to buy it?"

"Wait," said Muller. "I'll answer both questions. But last first . . . "

The young men listened. In his marked German accent, Arnulf spoke with quiet assurance:

"Regardless of what is written on deeds remember this: God owns the land. Not me, or you. We are only His administrators, here for a time to take care of it. The grass, plants, trees, the animals; they are His creation. We have always to remember that. It has been my guiding principle for living."

The young men shifted uneasily.

"You've seen my farm," continued Muller. "Now I must explain some other things . . ."

It was difficult for Muller, without boasting, to tell it. But he wanted the boys to understand.

As a boy in Lubeck, Germany, Arnulf favored engineering. Then the possibilities of power applied to agriculture captured his imagination. He went to work on a farm during the summers, and kept this up until he had completed his first two years of college.

In 1928, with the encouragement of a friend who had already crossed the ocean, Arnulf Muller put $25 in his pockets and headed for America, determined to finish his agricultural education. Upon arrival in New York, unable to speak English, Muller sought out his friend who was working on a country estate near New York City. Arnulf was hired as a farm hand.

"But the tenant farmer was not a born cultivator of land or caretaker of animals," said Muller. "He was in the farming business to make money only. I was a little too outspoken and soon found myself hitchhiking on the road. But I felt tremendously free and relieved."

Muller heard of a German-speaking foreman on the "Emmadine" farm near Hopewell Junction. He asked there for a job.

"How much do you want?" asked the foreman of J. C. Penney's Guernsey breeding farm.

Muller told him he was only interested in how much he could learn. Said he figured they'd pay him what he was worth.

"I'll put you on," the foreman told him. For the first two months he worked 10 hours a day—spreading manure.

Soon Muller became the regular relief man, rapidly learning every man's job of the 30 employed at Emmadine. Within six months he was the second highest paid man on the farm. Gradually, too, he was learning to speak English and to know America.

Muller liked farming in New York State but wanted to make sure before settling down. Quitting his job, he set out in the Model-A to see what America looked like. But nowhere did he find land that attracted him like the trees and stone-fenced fields of the Berkshire foothills.

The tenant farmer, for whom he first worked, had meanwhile gone broke during the first stage of the depression and quit. The estate owner wrote Muller offering him management of the farm.

"Here was my second big break," Muller told the student group. "The owner was a fine gentleman and a banker. Even so, he understood when I told him good farming was not 'the more you put into it, the more you take out,' but was a combination of right practices, at the proper time and good judgment.

"The next eight years were probably the hardest of my life," continued Muller. "Here was a totally neglected and mined-out farm. It was a challenge to me, and I poured in sweat and blood. Eventually, through crop rotation and careful fertilizer practices, we did build that farm up."

"You did all right by yourself," one of the students told him.

"I was not exactly alone," Muller said, and blushed. "You see at this time there was a very pretty girl at the farm—Hedwig Ising. She came from the Rhineland. Naturally we . . ."

"Naturally," agreed the students, grinning. Muller joined in the laugh.

"But when did you buy *this* farm? You haven't yet told us how it's done without dollars!"

"I'm just coming to that," said Muller.

One day, deciding it was time for a change, he wrote to a local real estate man, saying he wanted to rent a farm of his own. A telephone reply told him that Mr. De Frane on Quaker Hill would consider renting his farm to him. Muller went to look at it.

What he found was an old New England type farm, developed by a New York businessman into a place of great charm. Large stone barn, ample rolling fields, a brook and some wooded hills. A dairyman's dream. Muller sighed and shook his head.

"It's bigger than I can afford. I'm just starting out on my own."

De Frane stopped him. "I've heard how you farm. Ever since I came out here, I've wanted this place run that way. We'll work something out. Is it a deal?"

Muller and Hedwig and their two young sons moved into the new eight-room tenant house, half afraid De Frane might change his mind. A long range plan was worked out for each field. Some steep acres were returned to forest use and replanted in young evergreens. A swampy pasture was drained by dynamite. The resulting six-foot-deep ditch became a brook, and the swamp a fine meadow. Contouring changed the appearance of the hill fields, and their productivity mounted.

One day four years later, De Frane told Muller, "Arnulf, I want to sell this farm to you. I think the man who farms the land should also own it."

Muller looked out over the fields without answering.

"I know what's on your mind, Arnulf; you haven't enough money saved. Well, why not try the bank?"

Mr. Holmes, President of a Pawling bank, listened to Muller's story.

"Nothing you can offer us, for security, is as good as what we know about you," he told Muller. "Your credit is good here for whatever you need."

When Muller took over the original 185 acres, they were producing only six cans of milk per day, and all of the grain fed had to be bought, a yearly cost of six to seven thousand dollars.

Now, ten years later, the farm is producing twelve cans of milk per day; he raises almost all his grain, all of his hay, and even has some hay to sell. This past year Muller has added another 165 more acres to the farm.

Muller works the farm himself, with only one hired man. Though, during school vacations, Ralph and Martin, his two oldest sons, help with haying and harvesting. Seven-year-old Peter, the youngest, collects eggs and feeds calves.

Arnulf Muller finished his tale. "You see, my friends, your reputation as a good farmer builds credit—credit that's not measured in dollars, but in faith—your faith in yourself and in the land which a wise God has given us to care for."

"I only hope I can do as well, Mr. Muller," said one young man, "but it's mighty hard work, all alone. And getting up before dawn every day in the year—that's terrible."

"It is hard work," replied Muller, "but it's wonderful. There's a hush at five o'clock in the morning. The world is a new creation, fresh and clean. When I go to the barn, my stock know me and they come and touch me with their noses. I feel their soft faces, and I feed them and they take the food from my hands, food which I got from God. That is my time of prayer, either in the barn, or, better still, out looking up at the hills. I don't kneel to pray, and I don't shut my eyes. I like to look straight up to God. He gives me the rain of summer and the snow of winter for my land, and He causes things to grow. He and I work together."

Muller glanced at the sky and then turned away.

"Come, it's time for milking. We'll go in the barn before you start for home."

Illustration, Arnulf Muller, see page 34

HOW

FAITH

ATTITUDES

INSPIRE

THE

CHAMPION

PAGE
92

PAGE
100

PAGE 84

PAGE 88

AGE 76

PAGE 81

THE INSIDE PITCH

by CARL ERSKINE

> *He once pitched a no-hit game against the Chicago Cubs—and struck out 14 New York Yankees in the 1953 World Series to set a new record. Here's the formula for victory by the ace pitcher of the Brooklyn Dodgers.*

WHY IS IT that two ball players with almost equal ability and potentialities can come up to the Major Leagues—then one succeeds, the other fails? I've spent seven years learning what usually makes the difference . . .

From the age of nine I dreamed of playing in the Major Leagues. Our all day family trips from Anderson, Indiana, to Cincinnati to see the Reds play were very important occasions. Mother would pack a lunch and she, Father, my two brothers and I would start at dawn, arriving in time to stand by the clubhouse door and watch the Major League players enter. How I yearned to be a part of it all!

My high school record as a pitcher, particularly the final game when I just missed pitching a no-hitter, brought me to the attention of Branch Rickey, then General Manager of the Brooklyn Dodgers. After a year in the Navy, an appointment was made for me to see Mr. Rickey. I was very nervous.

He asked none of the questions I expected. One of the first was, "Do you go to church?" I told him about my activities in the Anderson Baptist Church. Mr. Rickey could well have been a philosophical Indiana farmer. He wasn't interested in my pitching statistics, but in my attitudes about life. "You may play only one year of baseball," he told me, "but you'll be doing something active the rest of your years. Remember, you'll get out of life just about what you put into it."

After signing a Dodger contract and competing one year in the minors, Mr. Rickey felt I could get extra experience by pitching in the Cuba winter league. I wanted to get married. When I told him about this, his eyes glistened with approval.

"Home town girl?" he asked. I told him that Betty Palmer and I had been going together since high school. He asked about our families, our ideas about children and a home, the end result being we got married a little earlier than planned and played winter ball in Cuba too.

In 1948 my dream seemed about to come true. I was brought up by the Dodgers and given a chance to start against the Chicago Cubs. I beat them 6-4, but in the seventh inning, while pitching to Bill Nicholson, something pulled in my shoulder.

"The starting job is yours if you can keep it," Manager Burt Shotten told me after the game. Twice more I started and each time won. But my shoulder still bothered me. Not wanting to complain about my arm, I tried to work out the soreness privately.

Then things started to go wrong. I got beaten a couple of times, lost my spot on the regular pitching rotation, and finished the year on the downgrade. The following year at spring training I was still below par, physically and mentally. Before the 1949 season started, I was farmed out to Fort Worth.

In the spring of 1950 the miseries came back worse than ever. This time I was farmed out to Montreal, the Dodger triple A farm club.

"You'll be back," Branch Rickey told me, looking through me with those steely eyes of his. But no one seemed to know what was wrong with my arm. I felt defeated and ready to give up.

One day while baking my arm under the heating lamp, a baseball enthusiast, Dr. Charles Le Tourneau, stopped by to chat.

"I'm an administrator at Queen Mary Veterans Hospital," he said. "I think we can help your arm."

Several doctors examined me, then suggested that I study films of my pitching motion before the injury and after. Result—we discovered that, to compensate for the original injury, I was throwing differently. Soon I was learning to pitch all over again —the way I had two years ago.

I then won six straight games for Montreal, while the Dodgers, meanwhile, were having pitching troubles. "Recall Erskine," was the suggestion made to Branch Rickey. An unusual series of Rickey interviews to newspaper reporters followed.

"I'm flying to Springfield to see Erskine pitch tonight," Rickey announced. He arrived, and I pitched my heart out, beating Springfield 3-1.

After the game reporters asked Mr. Rickey if he would now recall Erskine. "I didn't see what I came for," the Dodger boss said, shaking his head.

Four days later Mr. Rickey announced that he was flying to see me pitch at Montreal. I gave all I had, and shut out Jersey City 5-0. Rickey again parried reporters' questions.

No, he wasn't ready yet to recall Erskine. "I really didn't come up here to see Carl pitch," he said, "I came up to see how he walked to and from the mound."

Reporters thought he was pulling their legs. He wasn't, of course.

"We won last night, didn't we?" I asked Betty, having read all this in the papers the next morning. I wondered what a guy had to do to get another chance in the Majors.

Five days later Rickey announced for the third time that he was flying to see me play. I was determined to pay no attention to it all. My arm felt good again, and I was learning how to pace myself better during a game. This time I pitched a second straight shut-out.

Several days later I was told to report back to Brooklyn. When I arrived in Brooklyn, Mr. Rickey called me into his office. "I think you have an explanation coming," he said, with a twinkle in his eye. "I knew weeks ago your arm was back in shape, but I didn't know whether you were in shape mentally. My trips and newspaper comments were to put as much pressure on you as possible." Mr. Rickey is tops when it comes to bringing out the maximum in players.

Once back in the Majors again, the big question was: could I stick? I began to concentrate much more on positive thinking. My prayers before a game now are not for victory, but that I be in tune with God's ways. If my mind gets a sense of rhythm and coordination, my body does too. Confusion and pressure then bother me less. If I neglect this meditation—call it an "inside pitch"—my mental conditioning is not complete.

Big crowds can put tremendous pressure on a ball player. In 1951 while pitching a game against the Cincinnati Reds, I had hurled seven innings of hitless balls when the thought of pitching a no-hit game began to excite me . . . too much. I started to worry, shook off a sign from my catcher, and Ted Kluszewski banged my next pitch for a clean hit. Bad thinking did this more than bad pitching.

One sermon has helped me overcome pressure better than the advice of any coach. Its substance was that, like a squirrel hoarding chestnuts, we should store up our moments of happiness and triumph so that in a crisis we can draw upon these memories for help and inspiration.

As a kid I used to fish at the bend of a little country stream just outside of my home town. I can vividly remember this spot in the middle of a big, green pasture surrounded by tall, cool trees. Whenever tension builds up both on or off the ball field now, I concentrate on this relaxing scene, and the knots inside me loosen up.

Marvin Rackley, my former Dodger roommate, conditioned his thinking by reading Scripture. He got me in the habit of packing my own Bible on road trips.

On June 19th, 1952 I started against the Chicago Cubs. It was a raw, windy day—the same team and the same type of weather as when I pitched my first Major League game six years ago and injured my arm. In the third inning it started to rain; time was called for 44 minutes.

When we resumed play, instead of worrying about my arm, or the fact that I had a no-hitter going, I tried to concentrate on the job at hand.

The ninth inning came, we led 5-0 and the Cubs had reached first base only once—on a walk. But I had been close to a no-hitter before. The first two men went out—one more. The count went to 3 and 2. Feeling the strain, I willed my mind and body to keep loose and coordinated. My next pitch was a curve, which Miksis hit on the ground to Reese for an easy out to first.

I know only too well that yesterday's no-hitter means little today. Or victories in the World Series—or strike-out records. Every day calls for a new effort. I have much to be grateful for, a lot to learn still, but I do know the most important asset a person can have—faith in God. It gives one faith in self and others. It's like a dynamo—it's the difference.

Illustration, Carl Erskine, see page 75

WHAT ARE WE MISSING?

by CLARENCE "BIGGIE" MUNN

> *"Americans are losing the art of enjoying the things that really count," says Biggie Munn, Michigan State's Athletic Director and former head football coach.*

I READ AN article recently which stated that Americans use 19 million sleeping pills a day, mainly to cure sleeplessness and headaches resulting from worry.

Why, I asked myself, are we Americans in such a state today?

We are prosperous, almost everyone has a job, and we have far more devices for amusement than any generation in our nation's history.

True, there is the atom bomb, yet I do not believe this is the real reason for the worry, unrest and unhappiness which is almost the trademark of our present era.

Are Americans losing the art of enjoying the things that really count? I think so.

It's my belief that man-made pleasures will never bring the deep-down satisfactions and tranquility which come from the basic things which God created for us to enjoy.

I am grateful I was born on a farm, and a small one. Cynics may gibe at the oft-repeated American story of the boy of humble beginnings who made good, but it will always be a thrilling theme to me.

When I was eight, I lost my father. My Scotch mother, doggedly determined to keep her family together, "took work out" as they used to call it in Minnesota.

My brother, two sisters and I joined with her to keep our family united and to fight the threat of hunger. I know Mother worried far more than we kids. How could she help it?

Still I don't remember her fretting nearly as much as I recall her great faith, her precious Bible and such favorite passages as— *Be strong and of good courage: Be not afraid, neither be dismayed: for the Lord thy God is with thee ... **

Such as this was the source of her strength and our oneness.

Were there any pleasures in this kind of existence? I answer emphatically—a great many.

Without actually realizing it, we developed a wonderful bond through family teamwork. One job I had while in high school, for instance, was digging basements, using a shovel, scraper and a team of horses. It was a tough test for a kid, but I got a real kick out of adding my pay to the family treasury.

Between such jobs as this, I did some running on the high school track team. Often I combined my outside chores with my speed trials. During my freshman year at the University of Minnesota, I was a car parker outside the stadium. I never even saw a college football game until I started as fullback for the Minnesota Gophers in my sophomore year.

Perhaps, because our family had so few material things to smile about, Mother always was cheerful.

"The most popular person is the one who is always smiling," she would remind us frequently.

Joy was not a product of some happy circumstance, but something to be cultivated—like a crop. And our life was zestful because we created joy within ourselves.

When I was a football coach I found this same idea helpful in preparing our Michigan State team for a new season. Football training requires painstaking practice and work. I am a stickler for this.

Yet I also believe in coaches taking time to inject a light touch by permitting some horseplay and kidding. I have found joy can have the therapeutic effect of unlocking tensed muscles and

* *Joshua* 1: 9

adding a certain buoyancy and rhythm to the performance of a team.

This was our family formula, which I adopted as part of my system of coaching. All of us who teach the youth of this country have unlimited opportunities to do so much more than just instruct them in proper techniques.

Along with blocks and tackles, I used to stress to my boys at Michigan State the importance of love of country, faith in its institutions and the religious base on which it all rests.

Michigan State players say a prayer before each game. Mind you they do not pray for victory, but for strength and courage and loyalty. They must go out and earn the victory by their own determination.

Along the way has come the know-how to put myself in my proper place when I begin to take myself too seriously. Rather than reach for an aspirin, I'll go outside, find a quiet spot and study a cloud formation; or perhaps concentrate on the shadings of a sunrise or sunset. Perhaps I'll be fortunate enough to be a spectator as a bird builds its nest.

Nature provides so many relaxing pleasures if we but care to take the time to see them.

When the pressures and demands on my time are keeping me away from my wife and children, in my schedule will appear such items as "June 1-8, Canada, Vera and Janey." and "Aug. 6-13, canoe trip, Mike."

Any busy man who doesn't give his family the same billing as a business trip is not giving himself, or his family, a break.

Out of my boyhood struggles and hardships have come a solid sense of values and an appreciation about what is worthwhile in life. I have tried in the best way I know how to communicate my faith and philosophy to my boys, to show them that there are no short cuts, no free rides, and that the hard way is the best way.

Illustration, Biggie Munn, see page 75

BEAUTY IS OF THE SPIRIT

by COLLEEN HUTCHINS

Miss America of 1952 always thought of herself as too tall, too skinny. Yet the philosophy of her mother, and the quality of her family life, helped Colleen Hutchins win the number one beauty achievement in America. And the kidding from her brother, Basketball Star Mel Hutchins, didn't hurt either.

As soon as I heard about my brother's award several winters ago, I called him in New York, where he was playing in the East-West basketball game as a representative from Brigham Young University.

"Mr. Mel Hutchins," the long distance operator said, "will you accept a collect call from Miss Hutchins in Salt Lake City?"

Mel, you see, had won a cup as the most valuable player in this game. Whenever he does something outstanding, it's sort of a standing gag that I telephone him collect, no matter where he happens to be.

"Congratulations!" I told him. We kidded around for a while, he being offhand and modest about his new honor as usual. Then he made this parting shot, "I'll get back at you in good time, just wait."

Mel, I think gets real humility from mother. She is completely calm and serene, at least on the surface, about the victories and defeats of her seven children. She and my father together have a deep religious philosophy that has laced our family tightly together over the years.

It is taken for granted that each member of our family plays an active part in the church. All my brothers have had, or will have, periods of training as missionaries—a general practice for young men in our church.

I have taught Sunday School for years. It is work I love; teaching youngsters the importance of their own religion is, in my opinion, essential to our national health and vitality as well as to the children's own well being.

Our family ties mean even more now that some of us travel so widely. A prayer bond does a lot to knit us together. Mother, for example, is so concerned about the speed of travel these days that I think her prayer reaches out to us on wave lengths.

Not so long ago, my younger brother, Gene, was driving across the Great Salt Lake Desert in Utah. This road is so straight and smooth that it is very difficult to keep the speed down. There was a blow-out. Gene's convertible turned over three times.

The next thing Gene knew he was lying on a strange bed, having great trouble breathing. He felt no pain, but told us later, "I simply knew I was going to die. There wasn't any question about it."

So badly hurt was he that those attending him gave up hope. Gene heard one of them say, "Call the boy's family first, the doctor won't do him much good now."

Unable to get to Gene fast enough, we telephoned several young Mormon missionaries to rush ahead to him. They arrived and began a prayer vigil. Gene did pull out of it, making a remarkable recovery.

Several months ago when I went back to Utah for a visit, I drove over the same road with some friends. As we drew near the scene of Gene's accident, I told the others what had happened. For some reason I slowed down.

Then I began to hear a peculiar noise; it seemed to come from the engine.

I am no mechanic; a noise is just a noise to me, but I did stop at the side of the road. The front wheel was slanting away from the hub at close to a 45 degree angle, the only thing holding it to the wheel base being a small groove, worn into the metal itself. We were chilled at the thought of what might have happened.

Now, I have usually shied away from modern stories of prayer miracles, but these experiences convinced me that we should never underestimate what God can do for us, or through us, if we believe in prayer.

My entry as "Miss Utah" into the 1952 Miss America contest was the subject of conversation, and a lot of kidding in our family. So lightly did I take my chances that I acquired tickets to a Broadway play the night after the Atlantic City contest. It didn't occur to me I couldn't use the tickets if I won.

Many people perhaps don't realize that Miss America selections today are based on three separate tests: the girl's talent, physical appearance and general intelligence.

The first night was talent night. I was grateful that my family had encouraged all of us to develop one field in which we could perform better than average. With me it had always been dramatics.

The second night of the contest was the traditional bathing suit stroll. Now all members of our family are on the tall side; I am 5 feet 10 inches in stocking feet. Too much stature may seem to be a disadvantage to girls, but despite the kidding around in our family, we're all secretly proud of our height.

The most interesting, and most serious, part of the pageant was held on the third night. Questions were asked of contestants who then had to answer with impromptu speeches.

"What do you think is the most serious problem that faces America today?" I was asked.

My answer: "Our relationships with foreign countries." I then went on to explain my belief that any problem can be worked out on the basis of religious principles. William Penn's statement,

"Those people who are not governed by God will be ruled by tyrants," makes my point for me.

While certainly no authority on foreign relations, I do believe that nations cannot rise higher than the standards by which their families live—certainly families with clear cut moral and spiritual codes have greater understanding, mutual respect and love.

When I called my mother to tell her that I was the new Miss America, I'll never forget her answer. I had to laugh, it was so typically mother.

"Well, goodness sakes, Colleen," she said, "What in the world did you win it on?"

Later, came the long distance call that I had been expecting. "Sit back and relax now, Miss America, for a nice long chat," Mel said. "This time you're paying for the call."

Illustration, Colleen Hutchins, see page 75

EVERY KID HAS HIS HERO

by **DOAK WALKER**

How does sports competition build outstanding citizens? Doak Walker, a famous football all-American at Southern Methodist and now a star halfback for the Detroit Lions, tells the heart-warming story of the boyhood influences which guided his life.

I HOPE THAT PARENTS won't discourage their youngsters from participating in sports just because of the publicity given to a few athletes who went off the beam in recent years. For every disgraced athlete there are thousands who, through their character and sportsmanship, are a wholesome influence on the youth of America.

I'm no one to preach a sermon, but I would like to reminisce on what my athletic experience has meant to me.

My father once told me: "Play football as long as you enjoy it, Doak. Play clean. When it's no longer fun, stop playing."

I'll probably always be a kid in my love for football. (I also believe that the professionals play ball because they like it. The pay helps, but the desire and love for the game is the main factor.)

As a boy I had my heroes. One was Harry Shuford, a great triple threat star for Southern Methodist from 1933-1935. In my grade school English class I wrote a theme about Harry, who, I pointed out, was great not only because of his ability, but because he had ideals and gave up individual honors to boost his teammates. I wanted to be like Harry.

My dad has always been a hero to me. As football coach at North Dallas High, he started tossing a football at me when I was 18 months old. When I was 3, I made my first trip to the high school locker room and immediately fell in love with the leathery, sweaty, locker-room odors. In the equipment room I put on a pair of football shoes, and clopped triumphantly around the room.

By the age of 6 I had learned to drop kick a ball over the clothesline in our backyard. My sister, Pat, would retrieve the ball, with our dog, Jakie, barking after her. More often, though, my kicks wobbled to the side and into mother's rose bed.

There was plenty of time for athletics in my young world, but my parents made it clear to me that sports were not the most important thing in life.

God had top spot in our family. We said the blessing before every meal and prayed together for many things—problems of the day, our family and friends . . . world peace.

Both mother and dad taught Sunday school in the Westminster Presbyterian church. I can well remember slipping out of my junior Sunday school room and into my father's class for older boys . . . to listen intently to his down-to-earth interpretation of Christian living.

Since it wasn't possible for me to have dad as my high school football coach, then I'm glad it was Rusty Russell. Rusty not only built strong teams, but his coaching program was aimed at promoting ideals and creating life-long friendships. One fall he had us camp together in the gym for two weeks before school opened. We practiced on the field, ate together in the school cafeteria and slept in the gym camp style.

It was during one of these nights that our squad got together and spent a lot of time and thought working out a set of football objectives. The seven rules we drew up included emphasis on sportsmanship, hard but fair play, learning to think, personal conduct on and off the field, knowing how to take defeat and the importance of scholarship.

Bobby Layne and I were co-captains of our high school team

that year. Bobby, one of the closest friends I ever had, went on to Texas University. A year later I went to Southern Methodist.

The college game which I will perhaps remember longer than any other was the one we played against each other back in 1947 in the Cotton Bowl. At game time both Texas and SMU were undefeated and untied. Bobby and I had been playing together since Junior High; now we would have a chance to match wits against each other in friendly rivalry. Layne had already become recognized nationally as one of the best passers in the game.

I did what I always do before the kick-off of every football game, I paused for a moment and said a short prayer—I prayed for Bobby, for all the players and asked that no one be hurt.

Texas kicked off to us. In a few quick plays we scored a touchdown and led 7–0. Then Bobby got his passing wizardry going and it was soon 7–7. Later in the game we scored again and kicked the point to make it 14–7. Bobby's passes netted another touchdown, but the all-important extra point was missed. We won 14–13.

It was one of those very exciting, rugged, but clean games that make competitive sports so stimulating for youth. Victories are wonderful and this one made me thank God for the exhilaration of just being alive. But you can't win them all, and the defeats, believe me, are good in teaching humility.

Bobby Layne and I now play professional football on the same team, the Detroit Lions. On Dec. 21, 1952, came a great thrill and victory for both of us. Bobby's passing paved the way for us to meet the Cleveland Browns for the professional football championship. We won the title game 17 to 7.

Every man has a right to work out his own life pattern and personal convictions. I have never been ashamed of my complete faith in God. It means too much to me. I do not drink, although I wouldn't ever try to force my conviction about it on others. Therefore, it was no problem for me to turn down a $50,000 radio offer from a beer sponsor. I'm not crusading against beer, but I don't see how alcoholic drinks can help me get any more fun and satisfaction out of life than I do now.

I wouldn't be human if I didn't say that I've loved the excitement of football. But the things that have meant most in the long run are the friendships gained, the sense of values learned, and the hope that perhaps in some way I've measured up to my boyhood idol, Harry Shuford.

Along the way have come some wonderful awards which I hope I have deserved. But, putting first things first, I'll never value anything more than this note from my mother.

"I have been proud of you as a football player," she wrote me one Christmas, "but I am more proud of you as my son in the home."

Illustration, Doak Walker, see page 75

TECHNIQUE FOR VICTORY

by JOHN SHERRILL

Shy, unpopular Ben Hogan was "through" as a golf champ back in 1949, his body smashed in a car accident. Reporter John Sherrill tells how it was, only a year later, that Hogan was able to rebound amazingly—on to new championships and to a popularity he would have never thought possible before.

BEN HOGAN once said: "Since I was knee-high to a stymie, I've had to fight for everything I got." His introduction to the game that made him famous illustrates this.

Born in Texas—the son of a blacksmith—Hogan was selling papers in Fort Worth's Union Station at the age of 12 when he discovered that caddies at a nearby club made 65¢ a round. He went after the job, not even knowing what "golf" was.

The boss caddy sized Hogan up, picked out another runt who wanted to work, and told them to scrap. The winner would get the job. Ben won.

A year later he decided to try the game himself. Hogan didn't have a natural swing. But he understood work, and the importance of detail. Commented one of his own caddies, "He will even memorize the grain of the grass if it will help his game." Hogan, the golfing machine, was born.

It was a plodding, mechanical, intellectual approach to the game that brought Hogan to tournament play, years later. "He swings with the business-like authority of a machine stamping out bottle tops," one reporter said. And Hogan himself, describing his swing, uses the tip-off phrase, "muscle memory."

To memorize a stroke muscle by muscle takes hours of solitary practice. Although these silent hours began to pay off in Ben's game, they also took their toll on his personality. Hogan became dour, taciturn. On the links he did not know how to handle the distraction of the gallery . . . their hero worship, jibes, requests for autographs. The only apparent solution was to shut himself off from the crowd.

These are not qualities to make a popular man, although they did make a champion. After a slow start, Ben, in 1945, began winning title after title. Outwardly the galleries did not like him. But there was something about the very shyness and metallic discipline of Hogan's personality that doubtless made many in his silent gallery say, "You know, I am probably the only one who does, but I like that guy, Hogan."

Then on the morning of February 2, 1949, as Hogan was driving to his home in Fort Worth, Texas, he was critically hurt in an automobile accident. The golf champion had a crushed pelvis, a fractured left leg, a crushed shoulder, a broken ankle, and was close to death from shock. Doctors hoped he would live, but doubted if he would ever walk again. Hardly anyone considered the idea that Ben might ever resume his golf career.

It wasn't much more than a year later that short, 130 pound Ben Hogan amazed the world by entering the Los Angeles Open —one of the top tournaments in the country. Although suffering from leg cramps, Ben limped to the first tee as the crowd cheered. Instead of the tense, fixed expression usually reserved for the galleries, Hogan's face broke into a warm smile.

Ben played his usual concentrated game, careful not to waste his energy during the 72 hole match. His courage and determination brought him a tie for the championship. He lost the play-off, but everyone was speaking of "Hogan's victory."

The performance was remarkable in itself but the change in the "Texas Iceberg" was talked about even more. Sports writers all over the country were asking: What happened to Ben Hogan during those months of rehabilitation?

When I met Hogan at the Hershey Country Club recently, I asked the golf champ this question, and found that the Hogans had received thousands of letters during this period of recovery, letters from all kinds of people—housewives, salesmen, office clerks, students, the man on the street—each with basically the same message: "You can win out, Ben. We'll be praying for you."

Hogan revealed that several things helped him during his recovery. His theory of muscle memory on the golf course had been simply this: if he practiced one shot long enough and with enough concentration, his muscles would memorize the shot so that it would become almost automatic. On his hospital bed, Hogan applied the same theory. If he concentrated hard enough on getting well—believed enough—and practiced this belief hour after hour—day after day—just as he mastered golf, so could he overcome physical illness.

"Before the accident I took things for granted, even such things as trees and grass—except when they got in my way for a golf swing," he admitted.

"But all the time I lay in my hospital bed, I didn't even take breathing for granted. Then the letters started to pour in, people writing me that they were praying for my recovery. This was something that had never happened to me before. I had always tried to shut myself off from spectators during a match so that I could concentrate on my game. Before these letters came, I told myself that I never cared much whether people were for me or against me.

"The prayers of these people—and those of my wife, Valerie—had a lot to do with my recovery. Their belief in me helped me believe in myself. I *had* to repay faith with faith."

Ben Hogan, my wife and I talked for over two leisurely hours. There was nothing cold or ungiving in his personality. He spoke eloquently of the people who had helped him, his wife's tireless patience, and his many new friends among the gallery, the sports writers and his competitors.

For a man considered "through" three years ago, one of sports' greatest comeback heroes has surely achieved amazing honors. In 1950 he won the U. S. Open. In 1951, he won the Master's, the "World's Championship" at Tam O'Shanter, and repeated his U. S. Open victory, spectacularly coming from behind to do it. The Philadelphia Sports Writers Association voted him the most courageous athlete of 1951; both the Professional Golfers of America and the Associated Press voted him 1951 "Golfer of the Year."

Hogan's technique of victory can be applied anywhere, by anyone, as Ben did both to golf and to personal problems.

Illustration, Ben Hogan, see page 74

HOW FAITH LEARNED AS A BOY GUIDED MY CAREER

by CECIL B. deMILLE

> *One of Hollywood's greatest pioneers and most famous figures found strength and guidance through his boyhood religious training. As a result Cecil B. deMille was inspired to produce such notable motion pictures as* Ten Commandments, King of Kings, *and* The Sign of the Cross.

YEARS AGO in New York city an interviewer approached me. "Mr. deMille," he said, "I want to ask you a rather personal question—a question which few interviewers may have asked you—but one to which many people would like an answer. *I want to know what the finest religious memory of your life has been."*

That one hit me squarely between the eyes. Religion has always been a vital part of both my home life and my career, but I was hesitant to discuss it openly. Still it was a good question, put differently by Thomas Carlyle. "The chief thing about a man is his religion."

I recalled my boyhood days when my father's vivid reading of the Bible had so profoundly influenced me. Then a particularly significant incident came into my mind . . . the occasion when a minister performed a complete church service with but a solitary boy in the congregation.

I never will forget this minister, with prominent red beard, who once came to preach for a week in my home town of Pompton, New Jersey. I was ten at the time. My father was one of the supports of our community church and acted as lay reader when the church could not afford a resident minister.

The visiting minister announced he would preach each day

during Passion Week at an early morning service—eight o'clock as I recall. The morning I planned to attend dawned cold and rainy. I walked alone to the church through a murky morning gloom. When I arrived I observed no one was present but myself and the red-bearded minister. I was the congregation.

Embarrassed, I took a seat, wondering anxiously what he would do. The hour for the service arrived. With calm and solemn dignity the minister walked into the pulpit. Then he looked down on me and smiled—a smile of great dignity and sincerity. In the congregation sat a solitary child, but he commenced the service as if the church was crowded to the walls.

A ritual opened the service, followed by a reading lesson to which I gave the responses. Then the minister preached a short sermon. He talked earnestly to me—and to God. When it came time for the offering, he stepped down from the pulpit and put the collection plate on the altar railing. I walked up and dropped my nickel into the plate.

Then he did a beautiful thing. He left the pulpit and came down to the altar to receive my offering. As he did this he placed his hand on my head. I can feel the thrill and sensation of that gentle touch to this day.

In walking back to my seat that day I knew this man's God was a real God, and that his faith was God-like in its monumental simplicity. It left a lump in my throat, and I cannot think of it even today without emotion. That was religion at its finest. It won my belief and strengthened my faith. I knew that the spirit of truth had been in that church with us.

This incident has had more recent significance. Many of us reach middle age and beyond, with the fear that our lives have been useless, wasted. Is it not possible that we—parents, preachers, teachers, writers, actors, editors, etc.—might have deeply influenced a child or grown-up as did the red-bearded minister?

Many of us have changed human lives for the better without knowing it. In moments of unhappiness and discouragement this thought helps sustain me.

When asked what it was that turned my mind toward the making of great Biblical motion pictures, I again trace back through the years to find the influence that first awakened my mind to the spiritual power of Biblical scenes. I have always been aware that the Bible was a "best seller," that more human beings have been interested in Bible stories than in any other stories on earth.

As a boy, however, I used to sit on the arm of a big leather chair every evening as my father read two chapters of the Bible, one from the Old Testament and one from the New. It was a family custom. My father, having been a writer of note in his day, read anything well, but he especially liked to read the Bible. He made the words come alive; the characters moved and breathed before our eyes. It seemed to us he touched the beauty and drama in every story, and our eyes glistened with excitement, then were wet with tears.

My father's great vulnerable point was that he loved to have his head rubbed. We children knew of this weakness and used it to our advantage. So absorbed did we become in the Bible stories that we hated to have him stop. So, I used to sit on the arm of his old leather chair, by pre-arrangement with the other children in the family, and rub his head as he read. So soothed and relaxed did he become that he would forget the hour and go on reading extra chapters to us as we sat intently around his chair.

I have no doubt that my father's vivid reading of Biblical stories planted in my impressionable mind a reverence and respect for the Bible, perhaps even a sense of its dramatic values, which in subsequent years was to turn me to the Great Book for themes to thrill motion picture audiences.

It was always a battle to get support and backing for Biblical pictures. Producers feared them on the basis such pictures would not yield enough to pay the enormous expenses involved. That was true with *The Ten Commandments, The King of Kings, The Sign of the Cross,* and *The Crusades.* However, they more than paid their way in both financial and spiritual benefits, and some are still playing in various parts of the world.

Years ago I heard of an interesting incident that occurred when *The King of Kings* was exhibited in Constantinople. A crowd of hoodlums came to the theatre to break up the show, and began by hooting and throwing things. In a few minutes the rowdyism stopped. The hoodlums were subdued by the beauty and sacredness of the theme. At the end they sheepishly admitted to the manager that they had come to scoff and— almost—remained to pray. A story of the incident was contained in an Associated Press dispatch.

I have been in Hollywood since 1913, during which time actors, actresses, directors and producers have passed in seemingly endless procession, some befriended by destiny, others lost in oblivion. In a maelstrom like Hollywood there are many reasons for failure and unhappiness. I believe the chief among these is the failure to realize that *the purpose of this life is understanding of the spirit and not worship before the calf of gold.*

Illustration, Cecil B. deMille, see page 74

THE PITCHER
AND THE PREACHER

by BOB FELLER

> *What happened when a baseball rookie of the Cleve-*
> *land Indians showed up for spring practice with a*
> *companion who was a preacher.*

I MET Charlie Fix shortly after I hit the big leagues. At that time I was a green seventeen-year-old kid in big-time baseball.

Charlie Fix was a young minister—tall, lithe, clean-cut, and a straight thinker—from my own home town of Van Meter, Iowa. He had a small Methodist Church there. Charlie had been good at sports in high school and college, and I remember that it came as a surprise to me to discover that a reverend could be both a man of God and a good athlete.

Our friendship grew, and in years that followed our paths were to meet frequently. At the start of my first full year in baseball, I invited him to come South to spring practice with me.

At this time I was—as far as the experienced veterans of the Cleveland Indians were concerned—"damp" behind the ears. Frankly, they were pretty much right.

For example, I had been told that everyone in baseball chewed tobacco. Since my stomach couldn't take tobacco, I chewed licorice.

When I arrived in New Orleans in the spring with my "Preacher Friend," the older men on the squad were contemptuous. When they discovered that I had dug up a uniform for Charlie Fix, they really sounded off.

"We're such a bad influence on rookies that Feller has to bring his preacher on the field to keep us in line," one veteran growled sarcastically.

"Remember, fellas, no swearing now...."

I listened with burning ears. I was worried, too, and the next day my worst fears were realized—some of the players were out to make Charlie look bad.

Charlie was invited into a pepper game. This is a form of limbering up where one man taps out a ball to four or five players. Only the balls hit to Charlie could hardly be called taps. I noticed with pride that he more than held his own. He looked as lean, as agile, and in as good condition as anyone else on the field.

Finally, one leathery old vet picked up a ball and glove and motioned to Charlie that he wanted to "toss a few." This pitcher —malicious and bad tempered—was a bear on young players.

No one paid any direct attention to what followed, but I think everyone watched out of the corner of his eyes. The two began by throwing leisurely back and forth. Then the hard-skinned old pitcher started to put some stuff on the ball.

"Smack"—came the crackling impact, and the young minister winced as he caught this scorcher. Charlie threw it back just as hard. A slow burn crept upon the old-timer's face. "The young upstart!" "Crack . . . crack . . . crack . . ." Back and forth the ball flew as the two tried to knock each other down.

Finally, the manager noticed what was going on and rushed over angrily. "Cut it out," he bellowed at his star pitcher. "This is spring training, not midseason."

But there was new respect in the eyes of the players for Charlie. And before the training season was over Charlie and the cantankerous pitcher were close friends. I was proud of him and glad that I had brought him down.

From then on, Charlie was a wonderful influence on me in so many ways. He never preached religion at me. To my questions about the church he gave straightforward answers.

"Bob," he said to me once, "you know, I'd like to have you join my church—or any church, for that matter. But it's your decision. I think a lot of your friendship and I'm always ready to help you in any way that I can."

That hit home. At a time when organizations and people were

really pushing me, Charlie simply offered friendship and help.

And everywhere he won the respect of persons who nourish the mistaken conception that ministers are stuffy, pompous, and physically inept.

We had just returned from a hunting trip one day to meet several reporters at the hunting lodge. As they crowded about with questions, I showed them my new rifle with a telescopic lens. Someone then placed a light bulb down the road a hundred yards or so. From where we stood it was just a small blob of light on a rock.

I gave the gun to the reporters and each tried it out. They shot holes in the nearby foliage and bounced bullets off the rock itself, but none came near the bulb.

"Give it a try, Charlie," I suggested. One of the reporters handed the gun to him gently and started to show him how to hold it, knowing that he was a clergyman. I chuckled to myself. Little did they know.

Charlie took a bead on the small white dot, pulled the trigger. There was a small tinkle and the light bulb dissolved. I looked with amusement at the surprised scribes, and chalked up another decision for Charlie.

Some time later I met Charlie in New York, where we were playing an important series with the Yankees. In the first game the New Yorkers belted our pitcher hard to win, with Joe Di-Maggio, their great outfielder, knocking out two home runs. Charlie viewed the game intently from a box which I had wangled for him.

"Know something?" he said after the game. "That DiMaggio murders a high inside fast ball." I didn't pay much attention, and soon we were discussing other things.

The next day was my turn to pitch. In the first inning Joe DiMaggio came up. I wound up and poured in my fast ball—high and inside. Joe stepped back, took a hefty swipe at it, and I sadly watched the ball soar out of the park for a home run. Then I remembered Charlie's words of the day before.

In the ninth inning I had a slim one-run lead. When Joe Di-Maggio came up again the crowd roared for him to duplicate his first-inning home run to tie up the game. I fired in nothing but low inside pitches and struck him out to end the game.

I have to chuckle every time I think of how it took a minister sitting in the stands to pass on a tip to a ball player who had trained for years.

Then there was the time in Des Moines when I was to speak on a radio program. When I arrived at the station, a man from an advertising firm asked if I would endorse his product. "We'll give you five hundred dollars just for your name," he told me.

Five hundred dollars was a lot of money to me then, but I didn't use the product. "What should I do?" I asked Charlie. "Five hundred is easy money."

He smiled. "You never use the product?"

"I don't even like it," I answered.

The decision was bigger than just a matter of money. Charlie knew it—and so did I. He wanted me to make the decision.

I told the advertising man I couldn't do it.

Another decision came the same slow, hard way. One Sunday morning in my home town my father, mother, sister, and I went over to Charlie's Methodist Church together. It was the day for taking in new members.

At the given time I went forward and stood in front of my stanch friend. Solemnly I took the vows and accepted the responsibilities that go with church membership—vows that I will try my best to live up to every day of my life.

Illustration, Bob Feller, see page 74

PAGE

PAGE 106

SEVEN

GREAT

COMEBACKS

PAGE 110

PAGE 114

PAGE 132

PAGE 128

PAGE 118

SPIRITUAL MUSCLE

by BABE DIDRIKSON ZAHARIAS

> *"Babe" had never been ill a day in her life. Then suddenly she was faced with a physical challenge— greater than any ever faced in some 334 athletic contests over a 20-year period.*

A LITTLE dazed, my husband and I left the doctor's office and walked through the streets of Beaumont, Texas, to our hotel. George kept saying: "Cancer? That's impossible."

It seemed impossible, for me. I had never been ill a day in my life. Years of athletics had practically guaranteed good health. I had just won the 1953 Babe Zaharias Open in Beaumont and was packed for an early start for Phoenix where I wanted a few days' practice before the next tournament. I had been feeling unusually tired, so George and I decided on the medical examination. Now I found myself headed, not for a golf tournament, but to the hospital.

Most dreadful was the thought that I would never again participate in sports. The most important part of my life was being slammed shut. From now on, I could only look back.

I could look back on the 1932 Olympics when I won two first-places—in javelin throwing and the 80-meter hurdles. I could look back on a 20-year career which took me into 334 contests in every amateur sport, and I had won all but two. And I could look back on golf, the game I loved, in which I had won every tournament it was possible for me to enter.

It was summer of 1952 when I became aware of a strange weariness. My drives were falling short. On the green, I missed easy putts. George sensed my doubts.

"This tiredness, honey," he said. "If it worries you maybe you ought to see a doctor."

Once we had the doctor's diagnosis, nobody made a secret of

the fact that I had cancer. I've never understood why cancer should be unmentionable. In golf, you know where the sand traps and water holes are ahead and you try to guide your shots accordingly. With cancer, you know that recovery will require something more than surgical skill, so—in a sort of spiritual way —you guide your shots.

Soon the newspapers everywhere announced that I had cancer. Thousands of cancer patients and thousands of others who were afraid of the disease wrote, wired and telephoned in the few days before my operation.

Everybody promised prayers.

This was something new for me. All my life, I had looked upon prayer as something very personal between God and me. I guess I've prayed for the same blessings and with the same gratitude as everyone else, but it never occurred to me that thousands of people, separated far from each other, could effectively join in a barrage of prayers for the sake of one person— for me.

Being an athlete, I could express my feelings by saying: "Here is wonderful teamwork in faith."

Many times after a tournament, I recalled, a fan would say something like, "My heart was in my mouth when you lined up that tricky putt on the 10th hole. I was praying all the time." Yet I didn't think anybody was really praying. Now, lying in the hospital, waiting for surgery, I felt differently. If I was going to be all right again, I'd need more than my own prayers: I'd need the prayers of everyone who had promised them.

Suddenly I looked upon prayers as muscles, and I realized that the strongest people in the world must be those who pray for each other. There was strength in this sharing, but I soon realized that I had to give to others as well as accept for myself. It would help us all move closer to God, "from Whom all blessings flow." * Praying for each other struck me as a spiritual training

* *From the Doxology*

which kept everyone spiritually fit to deserve those blessings.

After the operation, the doctor came to me. "All right, Babe," he said, "I want to see you up and out of here real soon, and before the season's over I want to read on the sports pages that you've won another tournament."

The doctor had performed a colostomy—surgery that meant vital changes in my entire way of life. People I had known with colostomies were virtual invalids. For a fleeting moment, I was terrified—until I remembered that I hadn't gone into this thing alone.

Many letters had come from people with cancer, people who seemed more concerned about my recovery than their own. One man wrote:

"You must return to your game, Babe. Knowing you're back at golf will be a victory for us, too. Cancer kills more than a human body; it kills the human spirit because we feel we who have it are incurable. Your physical recovery, Babe, will provide a spiritual steadiness for all the rest of us. That's why our prayers are always with you."

Suddenly I realized that golf now for me was more than a sport. Because of what it would symbolize to thousands of cancer patients—a victory through spiritual strength—my game would become, in a way, a symbol of faith.

A few months after the operation, I stepped up to a tee for the first time. Despite my confidence, I couldn't suppress a small uncertainty. I was anxious for the first shot, yet a little afraid of it.

I swung. When I looked up I saw the ball arching far down the fairway. I glanced at my husband. He was smiling.

Now there was a job to do. First, the doctor's prescription: Play Golf. And there were the cancer patients, many of them with colostomies, who were looking to me for the same help I had received from them. Knowing now that God answered prayers, I wanted to return to golf to demonstrate this—and also to show others that they, too, could resume their normal lives.

In August, 1953, just four months after my operation, I entered Chicago's Tam O'Shanter Tournament. Back amongst the best players in golf, I was keenly aware of the competition. Tenseness tired me quickly. I began missing easy shots.

We were on the fifth green when an important putt stopped just short of the cup. Shattered, I stretched out my hands, still gripping the club, and buried my face in my arms and cried. This was my blackest moment, even worse than learning I had cancer. The tournament had taken on a special meaning, and there were thousands of others, I felt, who would be on the losing side with me.

Standing there, so terribly alone, I heard George approach me, and Betty Dodd, my playing companion. I felt their comforting hands on my shoulder—and, in a wonderful way, the hands of the many others. I whispered.

"Please, God . . . You've helped me this far. Give me the strength to go on . . . please."

I came in third in this tournament, better than anyone expected. In quite a different way, I scored a first.

Somewhere between that fifth hole and the last, I made up my mind that there would be no more tears. Perhaps, for the first time, I really flexed my spiritual muscles.

A few months later, I won the Serbin Invitational; then the Sarasota Open and last spring the National Capitol Women's Open.

And this past July, I came out on top in the United States Women's Open, the most important tournament of the year.

Actually *we* won it.

We are the thousands of people whose faith helped make me strong. United through our prayers, we share our separate victories.

Illustration, Babe Didrikson Zaharias, see page 104

THE LAST ESCAPE OF MR. JAILBREAK

by **BILL ALLISON**

Here was one man nearly all prison authorities agreed was completely past hope and reclamation. His many escapes earned him over 100 years in sentences. Then an incredible thing happened.

FORREST TURNER was 19 in 1934 when one afternoon in Atlanta he accepted an invitation to go for a drive with a friend. Police stopped the car and identified it as a stolen vehicle.

Turner was terrified. He was working as a soda jerk at the time, supporting his widowed mother and a large family. He had no money for a lawyer, and no one would listen to his plea of innocence.

The court appointed a lawyer for him, a man who would serve without fee. Believing that since this was Turner's first offense he would merely be put on probation, the lawyer advised him to plead guilty. Obeying, the boy was stunned by the judge's stern:

"Four years in prison!"

Shocked and frightened, Forrest Turner turned quickly and knocked down the court bailiff. He raced from the courtroom, fled down seven flights of stairs and rushed out the back door. There he plunged into an open coal pit.

Startled workmen, shoveling a coal supply into the basement, heard the court bailiff's scream:

"Kill him; Kill him!"

They began beating him with their shovels. Turner scrambled out of the coal pit and rushed down the street—into the arms of a policeman.

The incensed judge sent the boy to the chain gang!

Long before I met Forrest Turner, I knew him by reputation. By the time he was 30, he had earned prison sentences totaling 100 years. As an incorrigible prisoner, he soon became known as Georgia's Number One Bad Boy.

Soon after joining the chain gang, Turner used a razor blade and black shoe polish to make a wooden pistol from an old orange crate. With it, he bluffed his way out of the prison camp. Captured immediately, he was given five more years.

Eight more escapes followed in quick succession, each adding their toll in prison years. Irked politicians, determined to lock Turner and his ilk away once and for all, approved a million dollar appropriation to build Tattnal Prison, acclaimed by all, when it was completed in 1938, as escape-proof.

Forrest Turner proved everybody wrong. Acquiring a box of automobile valve-grinding compound and a piece of piano wire, "Mr. Jailbreak" patiently and cautiously spent months cutting through the bars of his prison cell.

One dark night in 1943, he left his cell and freed two other prisoners. The trio took over the prison switchboard. They systematically called for guards to be sent to various parts of the prison, ambushed them and tied them up. Thus they took control of the prison and with 43 others escaped in a truck.

Captured a few months later, Forrest Turner found himself facing a prison life of 128 years. He and a dozen others were assigned to the infamous eight-ball squad, where, with huge iron balls chained to their feet and their hands in manacles, they spent their days digging up giant tree stumps.

This was Turner's darkest hour. Certainly there was no hope for him. He could expect no sympathy from the state, and his years among criminals had made his heart a concrete block of bitterness. There was nothing that could be done for him and nothing he wanted done.

God's blessings, however, do not always wait to be requested. To win our love, God does not hesitate to offer His.

Blessings came to Forrest Turner on two unrelated paths. First, his antics had brought prison life to the attention of every Georgia citizen. Aroused people demanded reforms. The pressure grew, until state officials appointed Wiley L. Moore, an Atlanta business man, as director of the State Department of Corrections. A believer in the latent goodness in every man, Moore extended to every prisoner a new chance for freedom. He unchained prisoners and made the eight-ball squad a thing of the past.

Forrest Turner was the first man Moore sought out.

"You are not a lost man," Moore said. "I can prove that by helping you find yourself."

These were bewildering words to a man who felt he had no reason to live. At first, Turner could discover no route out of himself.

But there was a second blessing speeding towards him.

Never, in all the years, had Turner's mother ceased her prayers for him. Knowing the injustice of his first arrest, she understood Turner's bitterness, his revengeful hardness.

More than she wanted his freedom, Turner's mother wanted her son to be once again the young man he had been, sacrificing himself willingly for his family. It was for this she prayed fervently.

When, after several conferences, Wiley Moore asked Turner which job he would like in the prison as part of his chance to live again, Turner asked if he could work in the dental laboratory.

After attending the prison religious service some weeks later, Turner returned to the dental laboratory where he suddenly dropped to his knees in the middle of the room and bowed his head. For the first time in years he prayed. Others in the prison were astonished, but Turner was aware only of an impulse he could not quell.

In 1946, Forrest Turner was transferred to the Fulton County Prison System, near Atlanta, where I am chaplain. Immediately, I asked that he be assigned as my assistant.

Everyone in Georgia had heard of the great change in Forrest Turner. Some didn't trust it. The distrust grew when news spread that Turner had appealed for a parole. Yet, when the parole board studied Turner's case, his miraculous conversion was not one of the factors considered. Reaching back almost 20 years, the board studied the facts of Turner's first arrest and realized the grave injustice done.

On March 4, 1949, I handed Forrest Turner the papers which made him a free man. Of all, I was the most anxious to see what would happen now to the religious life he had appeared to accept so completely. For a week I waited in silent fear.

Then came a telephone call. "I'm speaking at a church tonight," Turner said. "I'd like you to be there."

I was there that night to listen to the conversion story of Georgia's Number One Bad Boy. And I was never prouder or happier than when Turner firmly announced, "My greatest moment came when I realized I could escape from everything except from God."

Illustration, Bill Allison (left) and Forrest Turner, see page 105

MY CAREER TOOK
A TOBOGGAN RIDE

by **ANN BLYTH**

*She was sledding down an icy hillside like a snow-
bird. There was a sickening crash, and a young actress faced the greatest crisis in her promising career.*

WHEN I was a very little girl I remember praying fervently
for a pair of red wings. After several days of watching and waiting I took my shaken faith and spread it out before my mother.

"Why?" I demanded. "Why don't I get red wings?"

My mother had, skillfully balanced with her sensitive Irish
wit, an enormous respect for a serious problem. Together we examined mine. "Faith, my darling," she told me, "is believing that
God is very wise. Wiser than you. Somehow you must be praying wrong."

As I grew older I was filled with gratitude that I need not
walk through life wearing red wings. But, I was equally grateful for her gentle lesson.

Mother worked very hard and her tiny body wasn't nearly as
big as her heart. Yet I never heard her complain. In our walk-up
flat on New York's east side she would jubilantly finish a batch
of ironing for her select Park Avenue clientele and call to us to
admire its crisp freshness. Sometimes it was a close shave when
it came to scraping together the money for my singing, dancing
and dramatic lessons but she never told me of it. Instead, she
let me know constantly that faith was the foundation for lasting
joy, the chief cornerstone for building a whole life.

She dreamed dreams about my wonderful future as an actress
and at eight, nine and ten, I began getting radio and stage bits.
When I tried for something better and failed, she would smile

her wonderful warm smile, put a pert new feather in my hat, and together we'd go to St. Boniface's to pray.

"Just have faith, my darling," she'd say cheerfully as we walked home in the fading light. "Something better will come." And it did. It came so fast it was like riding a giant roller coaster clear to the top. We two looked out over the whole world. At thirteen I was on Broadway as Paul Lukas' daughter in "Watch on the Rhine." At fourteen I had dinner at the White House. At fifteen I came to Hollywood and was given the coveted role of Joan Crawford's daughter in "Mildred Pierce." Overnight life was glamorous, exciting, completely wonderful.

Yes, we went up so fast that when we hit the first giant dip it shook my faith. But it didn't shake my mother's on that tragic day in a hospital room, where doctors told me I might never walk again.

We had finished "Mildred Pierce" and Mother took a group of us to Snow Valley, a spot in the San Bernardino Mountains. While my friends and I were tobogganing, it happened. One minute we were sailing down the hard-packed icy hillside like snow birds, then there was a crash and I fell on my back with a sickening thud.

I didn't cry out. The feeling was too big for that. Involuntarily, from long habit, my spirit reached out for faith and halting prayers rose to my lips. At the hospital the doctors were grave; my back was broken.

My glowing world tumbled all about me! It seemed like the end of everything.

At first I couldn't look at my mother. When at last I raised my head, I was startled. Those warm hazel eyes under her crown of auburn hair were actually smiling.

"Have faith, my darling," she said. "You'll walk."

Together my mother and I planned cheerful, busy days. In a

cast, with my head and feet toward the floor, my back raised high, I concentrated on high school work, determined to graduate with my studio class.

But still there were those long periods of just lying there. The busy exciting world I had known faded away and my life slowed down to little things. But even here I found myself blessed, for a new sense of prayer began to unfold to me. Now there were not the busy times of telling Him what I needed but, rather, times of listening communion, of gathering strength, when my human strength and courage seemed to ebb away.

In seven months they told me I could walk. Not walk really, but take those first important few steps on the long road back to complete freedom. As I had gotten to know Him in my time of trial, I knew Him now in thanksgiving.

I took those steps, and then more. I graduated with my class from a wheel chair.

There were seven months in and out of that wheel chair, but every one was another step forward. There was my first swim. The preview of "Mildred Pierce." My first game of golf. And then I made my first picture since the accident.

Now, at last, life was again the same. Only, not quite the same. I found within me an immense gratitude for simple things. An acute appreciation of all I might have lost, all the things I had accepted unconsciously before. And one more difference, I had grown up. At first I had clung to my mother's faith, leaned on her, step by step as she showed me the way. Now, I had found my own rock. Nor did I find it too soon.

Before I finished that first picture after my accident I was standing alone. My mother, beloved companion, was gone. A little unsteadily I clung to my rock.

But I missed her. There was an aching emptiness. Until it came to me, almost in a revelation, that she had not left me. She had prepared me for her going as she had prepared me for everything else I'd met in life.

Reaching out again for my faith came the assurance that she would be by my side in every good, beautiful and true experience, wherever I might go; a part of every decision, every success and every happiness—for they all stemmed from her inspired teaching. They would become the flowers of the mustard seed of faith she had placed in my heart.

Illustration, Ann Blyth, see page 105

A FEW HITS FOR DAD

by **MICKEY MANTLE**
as told to Ben Epstein

Mickey was 15, his Dad 35, when they played to-gether on the same ball team. So starts the story of a rare partnership which brought the boy through crushing tragedies to triumph as a Yankee Stadium star. A truly moving story for every American fa-ther and son.

ONE APRIL DAY in 1953, I knocked a baseball out of Griffith Stadium in Washington, D.C. I'll not try and kid anybody by saying I didn't realize it was a long home run.

My teammates beat my back black and blue and "atta boyed" me all over the place. They compared the drive with ones slugged by Babe Ruth, Lou Gehrig, Ted Williams, Joe Di-Maggio and big people like that.

My folks back home in Commerce, Oklahoma, soon heard about it. When Mama telephoned that night, I gabbed first with her, then with my wife Merlyn, my three brothers, kid sister, and the neighbors who happened to drop in.

Frankly, I liked all these goings on, and there was no sleep in me that night. So I tuned in several sports programs, and they were talking about my homer. Then one announcer made me cry.

He mentioned my dad, Elven Charles "Mutt" Mantle.

This broadcaster recalled how my Dad taught me to hit both lefty and righty at the age of five, and how he raised me to be-come a professional ball player. What he didn't tell was how Dad tried to teach me to be a Big Leaguer off the diamond as well as on it.

While he was alive, I was Dad's life. Now, making good for Dad is my life. I guess that sounds a little strange, and maybe it is. Perhaps it may also sound strange that I still talk to "Mutt" Mantle, my father. That night in my hotel room I asked him:

"How about it? They say it went 565 feet."

Dad liked it but he wasn't satisfied. Now, don't get sore at him. He was just that way; he always demanded that I do better.

"It should have gone 600 feet," he said . . . inside me.

"Okay, okay, give me time," I said, and I'm sure he grinned.

I recalled when Dad drove me back home from Joplin, Mo., after I completed my first full year in the Class C Western Association. That was in September of 1950, and I was feeling pretty good for an 18-year-old. I batted .383, was plenty swelled up about it, and so began fishing for a compliment.

"How about the .383 average, huh?"

Dad never took his eyes off the road. "You should have hit .400," he said. And I thought I saw him grin just a little then too.

Demanding better than good was Dad's way of telling me there's always a bigger Umpire than the man in blue on the field, and He's the real judge of what you do. My father tried to model my baseball techniques from the start as a writer works on a novel, or a composer on a symphony.

I was named Mickey Charles; Mickey after Mickey Cochrane, the great Philadelphia Athletics catcher, and Charles after my grandfather. Dad and Grandpa both played sandlot baseball.

According to Mama I was in the cradle when Dad asked her to make a baseball hat for me. When I was five he had her cut down his baseball pants and sew together my first uniform. He labored practically all his short life as a lead and zinc miner.

Anyway, I was five when he began teaching me how to switch-hit.* Dad was a left-hander; Grandpa, a righthander. Every day after work they'd start a five-hour batting session.

Both would toss tennis balls at me in our front yard as hard

* A batter who can hit left-handed against right-hand pitchers, and vice-versa, has a big advantage.

as they could. I'd bat right-handed against Dad, and switch to left-handed against Grandpa. A grounder or pop-up was an out. A drive off the side of the house was a double, off the roof a triple, a homer when I hit over the house or somebody's window. I'm probably the only kid around who made his old man proud of him by breaking windows.

Dad hammered baseball into me for recreation, sure. But it was more than that. He was teaching me confidence by having unlimited faith in me. Dad was 35 and I was 15 when we played week-ends for the Spavinaw, Oklahoma, team. He pitched and I played shortstop.

Those games are the most cherished of my life. Bigger than any World Series. Why? Because we played together, and I watched Dad's faith in action. He was never angry. He was always patient. He was unhappy when anybody made an error, even on the opposing team. He didn't try to outshine everybody else. He just tried to shine in himself.

In high school he wasn't happy about my playing basketball and football too. During the scrimmage one afternoon I got a kick in the left shin. I hardly noticed it, though I did limp home.

The next morning my leg was twice its normal size and discolored. There was no x-ray equipment in Commerce, so Dad borrowed the money, and got me to a specialist in Picher, Oklahoma. On the way I could see him sort of whispering to himself. He was praying.

The doctor diagnosed my trouble as osteomyelitis, a bad bone disease.

Dad borrowed up to his neck and hustled me to a clinic in Oklahoma City. There was even talk the leg would have to be amputated. When I thought it would make me give up baseball I almost went crazy. More for Dad's sake than mine. But Mama, Dad and Grandpa all hung on. They made me hang on.

Know what saved that leg?

Prayer and penicillin.

When I got to recovering real good, I began swinging a sledgehammer at odd jobs and worked in the lead and zinc mines with Dad to put on weight and muscle. In a little over a year, I added eight inches and 40 pounds. One day in 1949, on the day I was graduated from high school, Dad said to me:

"Get me a few hits for a graduation present."

I sure tried, and I got him a single, double, and a homer.

Dad didn't tell me that a New York Yankee scout named Tom Greenwade was out there watching. After the game, I was signed first to the Independence, Kansas team, then to Joplin, both Yankee farm clubs. During the 1951 spring training season, I was brought up for a try-out with the Yankees!

Here was the chance to show everything Dad taught me. But how my teeth rattled! And how hard it was to control my anger. If I'd go without base hits for several days, I'd smash my knuckles against the concrete wall in the dugout, or hurt my toes kicking the water cooler. And after the game I'd ask Dad:

"What's the matter with me? What do I do wrong?"

"Bottle up your anger, boy," he'd say. "Let your bat do the talking for you."

That's the way he always was. Gentle and patient.

I started the season as a right fielder for the Yankees. I'd flash sometimes, more often I fizzled. Then in a double-header at Boston I struck out five times in a row.

I cried like a baby. "Put someone in my place who can hit the ball," I blubbered to Manager Stengel.

Soon after this I was shipped back to Kansas City for more "seasoning."

"I guess I don't have it as a Big Leaguer," I told Dad when I met him in Kansas City. "I belong in the minors."

First he whispered silently to himself, and then he said: "Mickey, things get tough at times and you must learn to take it. If that's all the guts you got, you don't belong in baseball."

His face was white and drawn. Dad had cancer, but I didn't know it.

He left. I stayed. I did some whispering too. On my knees. And I dug in. I got to hitting again. Before the season was out Mr. Stengel brought me back to the Yankees.

Seeing me start in the World Series was probably the proudest moment of Dad's life. In the second game I fell chasing a fly, ripped the ligaments in my right knee, and had to sit out the Series in a hospital bed. But it was all right. Dad was with me. He left a sick bed to see the Series.

"My back is acting up," he alibied, "but now I have to watch that knee of yours."

Then a doctor in the hospital told me Dad had cancer.

I guess I really woke up after Dad died. I mean I really got his message. Not because I had the responsibility and became the head of the family, looking after my mother and brothers and sister, and my wife. I guess I woke up to what he meant to teach me all the time. And I thank the Lord for Dad even though He did take him away at the age of 40.

There's a Micky Mantle, Jr. now. He doesn't know it, but he owns a ball, bat, and glove. It's all right with me if some more little Mantles come along in the future.

And some day I'm going to build a baseball park in Commerce, free to all, for every kid in town. It will be named Mutt Mantle Field, a sort of shrine for my father, who is still teaching me how to be a Big Leaguer—in the real sense.

Illustration, Mickey Mantle, see page 105

FACE TO FACE
WITH GABRIEL

by DR. MORRIS KERTZER

> *The crack Red Arrow Express was speeding to New York when it plunged into a ravine. Passenger cars were scattered about like toy trains. Out of the disaster has come an unforgettable story of personal courage and heroism.*

IT WAS the kind of snowy, windy night when movie houses are half empty, dates are called off and most people settle down in their easy chairs after dinner, happy to be warm and comfortable and at home.

But at the McKinley Avenue Reform Temple in Canton, Ohio, the pews were filled to overflowing this night of January 6, 1950. The entire congregation as well as many who were not regular worshippers—Orthodox Jews and Christians alike—braved the blustery weather to attend the services. For it was the first time in 35 months that George Lieberman, beloved rabbi of the temple, was to ascend the pulpit.

It was a tense, agonizing moment for every man and woman in that synagogue. Rabbi Lieberman moved slowly down the aisle, every step filled with pain. The congregation followed each faltering step breathlessly, aware that they were witnessing a great personal struggle. What flood of memories must have raced through George Lieberman's mind as he made the effort to resume his work—a comeback no one had dared hope for . . .

One February night, three years before, George and Sylvia Lieberman caught the crack Red Arrow Express, bound for New York. They were fast asleep in their berths when suddenly, without warning, the train shuddered violently, left the tracks and plunged into a deep ravine. Half a dozen passenger cars were scattered over the hillside, like a toy train tossed in all directions by a youngster at play.

Rabbi Lieberman was in Upper 6 of a Pullman coach. When the train catapulted, his berth snapped shut, trapping Lieberman with his legs inside the jammed compartment and his body hanging, head down, in the aisle.

The pain and the shock brought immediate unconsciousness. When he came to, there were moans and shrieks—and utter darkness. He shouted his wife's name, but there was no answer. He did not know that the car had buckled and Sylvia Lieberman had been hurled to the other half of the Pullman car, badly bruised, but safe.

He groped for some way to change position, perhaps to raise his head. After much fumbling, his fingers came upon the little net hammock, found in all berths to hold the traveler's personal effects. Painfully, he shifted his body so that his head rested in the hammock. Knowing that his spine injury would be aggravated without some support for his back, Rabbi Lieberman also managed, with the aid of a fellow passenger, to pull some suitcases and bedding under him, so that he could achieve a small measure of relief, while waiting for the rescue squads.

Someone called for a match. George Lieberman felt pillow feathers on his face and around his head, and his reaction came almost as a reflex.

"Don't light a match or we'll all burn! Spread the word around—don't light a match!"

Through the car, and then through the other coaches, the warning echoed: "Don't light a match!" The rabbi's presence of mind saved the wreckage from becoming a flaming death trap for all of his fellow passengers.

Others among the injured and the dying heard that there was a rabbi in their car, and called on this man of God to pray. Over the sound of the moaning and the tears, the calm voice of the rabbi was heard, repeating the familiar words of the Psalms: "Yea, though I walk through the valley of the shadow of death, I will fear no evil: for thou art with me."

Just a few hours before, the rabbi had been talking abstractly about interfaith understanding, respect and good will at a Brotherhood Week meeting in Canton. Now, men of different faiths were knitted together in a common bond of suffering, fear and disaster.

A Catholic, who lay dying, asked the rabbi to help him make peace with God. A Protestant, petrified with fear for his loved ones, took new courage from the measured phrases of a rabbi's prayers. Lieberman, in such unbearable pain that he occasionally blacked out for minutes at a time, forgot himself as he forced his weary voice to bring solace to those around him.

Slowly the work of removing the dead and the injured got under way. There were 25 dead, 100 injured. Some six hours after the wreck, the salvage crew reached the rabbi's berth. "There are six dead and one living right here," a man called out.

"One living!" George Lieberman caught the phrase. "They mean me, I guess."

The rescue men set to work on the locked berth. The tedious work of prying the rabbi loose took almost half an hour. For a while it was thought that his legs would have to be amputated to release him.

As his closest rescuer labored with his tools, George Lieberman tried to remove some of the tension under which he worked. "What is your name, my friend?" he asked.

"Gabriel," came the casual reply.

"Gabriel!" the rabbi whispered, half in jest, half in delirium. "Are you from here or from up there?"

The six-hour ordeal in that locked Pullman berth left the rabbi's legs paralyzed. Some of his doctors held out little hope that he would ever leave a wheel chair. Without the wonders of modern science, he could never have survived.

But medicine alone did not work this miracle. It rested heavily on Lieberman's indomitable courage and spirit—a spirit kept buoyant during weeks and months of pain, uncertainty and disappointment, by the unfailing love and affection of all with whom he came in contact.

In Mercy Hospital, in Altoona, where Rabbi Lieberman spent the first frightening, agonizing weeks after the wreck, there was the warmth and kindness of the nursing sisters. "A challenge has been placed in our hands by Jesus to keep a rabbi alive," they told him . . . and it was a challenge they spared no effort to meet.

And later, as weeks became months and months years, when even as strong a spirit as George Lieberman's was tempted to give way to despair, there was the faith of his congregation to sustain him. For they waited patiently, making no effort to replace him, certain that one day he would return.

And from the very first day of the accident, his congregation of well-wishers had mushroomed to include the entire community of Canton. Christians and Jews alike sent gifts and letters to Lieberman's bedside to wish him well and tell him that he was not alone.

During these years, Rabbi Lieberman learned also the brotherhood of suffering as he brought solace and hope to others in the hospital. He wrote to a friend: "Even when submerged in a whirlpool of hot water, in a cast, in a wheel chair or on crutches, undergoing physical therapy or secluded in a hospital room, I can carry on my ministry."

Lieberman often wondered where his rescuer, Gabriel, could be found. Gabriel's employers, the Pennsylvania Railroad, with only his first name to go on, one day traced him to a Cleveland hospital, where Gabriel lay seriously ill. Rabbi Lieberman made the painful trip to visit and comfort his rescuer, grateful for the chance to be of service.

Finally, on a cold January night back in 1950, Rabbi Lieberman made the attempt to preach in his own temple for the first time in three years. A steel brace supported his back, another brace lent strength to his legs, as he inched his way to the center of the pulpit and eased himself into a specially constructed device which made him appear to be standing, though he was sitting down.

In one of the front pews, his wife nodded to him with a smile of encouragement. The congregation arose to chant the *Shema,* the ancient Hebrew affirmation of faith.

Rabbi Lieberman then thanked the good people who sat in the pews before him. "What," he asked in his sermon, "are life's most precious possessions?"

He spoke of simple things, homely matters, things we take for granted like the air we breathe.

Speaking in the shadow of thirty-five months of nightmarish suffering, the rabbi concluded: "Whatever the circumstance, the crisis, the pain and the failure, whatever 'the bludgeoning of chance,' do not give up. Hold on! Live on! And pray!"

The prayers were ended and the rabbi intoned the benediction: "The Lord bless you and keep you; the Lord cause His spirit to shine over you and be gracious unto you; may the Lord lift His spirit upon each and every one of you, and grant you peace. Amen."

The congregants filed past the rabbi as they left the sanctuary. "Good Sabbath, Rabbi. Good Sabbath, Mrs. Lieberman. Welcome back."

George Lieberman had come home.

Illustration, George Lieberman, see page 104

LAND AHEAD!

by FLORENCE CHADWICK

> *Chilled to numbness by hours swimming the English Channel, Florence wanted to give up. But then her father, in the boat beside her, said something which changed everything. Don't miss this warm, human story of triumph over failure and fear.*

WHEN I STARTED out to swim the 21-mile channel from Catalina Island to the California Coast conditions didn't seem too different from my other swims, except for two things. I missed my father a lot, and we knew that an attempt was being made to televise my effort to be the first woman to swim this California Channel.

Fifteen hours, 55 minutes later, they pulled me from the water. I was just a mile away from my goal. It was the first time in my life I had been forced to quit.

It wasn't until some hours later, when the numbing cold in my bones began to thaw, that I really felt the shock of failure. When a sympathetic young reporter came to talk with me, I told him honestly, "Yes, I was cold. No, I wasn't tired."

Then, because he looked understanding, I blurted out what was secretly in my heart. "Look, I'm not excusing myself. But if I could have seen land, I might have made it."

Was that wishful thinking? The big "if" we all have afterward? Not entirely. When I first swam the English Channel in 1950, I thought I had gone as far as humanly possible. I was cold then, too. I asked to be taken out of the water.

Just then my father sighted land. He pointed. I saw it too. Land in sight! The thrill of that brought the warmth I needed and victory was sure. It didn't take much faith to swim on toward a destination I could see so clearly.

But the California Coast had been shrouded in fog that 4th of July morning back in 1952. Even the boats in our own party were almost impossible to see. When my mother and my trainer told me we were in sight of shore, that only fog obscured our landing place, I thought they were only coaxing, only encouraging me. I didn't believe them. I couldn't see it. And I was so cold.

True, I did wish for my father, who had passed away in November 1951, but the best part of him, his sure strong faith, had been with me in that 48 degree sea. The same prayer for strength and courage we always made together when I entered the water, I had made alone. Tired as I was at the end, I thanked God for my blessings as Dad had taught me to do when each swim was completed.

So, even though I knew I would try again, this first failure was a blow. Then I remembered my father and his saying that "good can come out of any experience if we enter into it with prayer and keep an open heart."

Well, I had entered this with prayer, and I was waiting, now, with an open heart to see what good could come of it. I didn't wait long.

Because of television, millions had seen the swim, some staying up on through the night. The flood of messages and some 3000 letters indicated they had seen much more in my long effort than I had.

There was a letter from a man and his wife, on the verge of breaking off their marriage, who sat in their living-room and watched me to the end. Something in the picture of a cold, lonely girl, swimming on and on through the night, touched them. "If you have the strength, the purpose and endurance to try that again," they said, "well, so have we."

A young man, who described himself as a tough, hard-boiled skeptic, wrote: "I never prayed in my life before, but when you were so close to shore, I found myself on my knees, asking God to give you strength."

This kind of response made me feel almost unworthy. None of my successes had ever won me so many friends. But the failure to swim a channel of water enabled me to learn something that will last a lifetime.

For reflection helped me see clearly that I had been licked by the fog. Like doubt, confusion or discouragement, the fog alone had no power to stop me. But because I let it blind my heart and reason, as well as my eyes, then it really defeated me.

I remembered that Jesus had said to one of His disciples: "Thomas, because thou hast seen me, thou hast believed. Blessed are they that have not seen and yet have believed."

At that moment I knew the real meaning of faith described in the Bible as, "the substance of things hoped for; the evidence of things not seen." When fog obscures our own vision, even when we've gone all out, and still seem to be failing and are too tired or cold to go on, then we must be willing to accept the word of someone who sees a little clearer, knows a little better than we do.

Realizing this made me accept my many new friends with a sure feeling that, fog or no fog, I wouldn't let them down again.

The day we picked for the second Catalina Island to California Coast swim was September 20th, over two months later. The weather was better, but we encountered many of the same obstacles as before. Three times sharks were sighted; members of my crew were forced to shoot several when they got too close. In the middle we came into such a bad patch of fog I could hardly see the boats, but I swam on.

My brother, for the first time, sat in the rowboat where my father had always been. When it was time for my nourishment, he elaborately put on a chef's hat, clanged a dinner bell and then fed me my four lumps of sugar. His humorous remarks, on the blackboard by which we communicated, kept my spirits high.

When I reached the California shore, breaking the men's record by nearly two hours, I was never so humbly grateful for victory.

But the joy of this triumph can not compare with the thrill I received from a letter sent me by one chronic invalid. Though depressed by a long illness, he had watched my first failure, and what he could see of the second success. He wrote how my effort had given him courage and strength to fight on. Even if he didn't see *his* goal of a complete cure, he had learned to have faith that for him, *somewhere,* there was . . . land ahead.

Illustration, Florence Chadwick and Father, see page 105

DISASTER CAN LEAD
TO VICTORY

by **HAROLD RUSSELL**

*When the shattering blast of a TNT block blew
off his hands, the paratrooper had moaned, "There
goes the great Russell." But how wrong! For scorn-
ing the use of artificial hands, Harold Russell mastered the art of using hooks . . . so well in fact that
Hollywood picked him for the role of Homer Parrish in the unforgettable film* The Best Years Of
Our Lives. *Russell's acting in this picture won him
two Academy Awards and national acclaim for his
courage in overcoming a serious handicap.*

IT SOMETIMES takes cold, black disaster to inspire one to achieve
the heights of success.

But for my accident I would now be back at my pre-war job as
butcher. Instead, I have been in motion pictures, on the radio,
subject of magazine articles—but best of all, I have had a chance
to show other disabled veterans like myself that it is possible to
bounce back from utter despair to undreamed of success and
happiness.

On that black June day in 1944 when I lay on a hospital bed,
looking down at two big bandages where my hands used to be, I
frankly thought it meant the end of useful living for me. What
can I do now, I asked myself bitterly? Probably just live out my
years on an Army pension.

This self-pity and despair didn't last very long though. There
is something in most people that won't let them take defeat lying
down. Call it anything you like, but to me it is *faith—faith* in
God and in myself, *faith* that I can always rise from every set-
back. A man is licked without this.

At Walter Reed Hospital there was no funeral atmosphere. Nobody pitied himself or anyone else. A guy with both legs gone was called "Shorty;" a man with but one leg, "Limpy;" and a soldier with only one arm, "Paperhanger." As for me—I was "Hooks." This may sound grim, but we had to develop a sense of humor, and this was the best way to do it.

My first reaction to the hooks, which were to serve as my hands, was one of dismay. The first day I tried them on, it was worse—it was torture. Unable to make them do anything, I was ready to give up. But the next day I tried again—and kept on trying until I made them work.

My first experiences out of the hospital were also trying ones. Those I met with a sense of humor were most helpful. Take the little old lady to whom I sold meat before the war. When she saw me, she broke out with: "Oh, you poor boy."

Then, realizing that this was the wrong approach, she stopped and chuckled, "No wonder you lost your hands. Goodness knows you sold them to me often enough weighing my meat. They didn't belong to you anyway; I bought them many a time with my pot-roasts."

I liked that reaction—frank and sassy.

The two chaplains in our hospital were two of the finest representatives of God I have ever known. They realized that it wasn't enough to simply tell us to have faith; we had to be shown how to apply faith in overcoming our handicap. In their talks with us these chaplains had many a sharp, realistic question fired at them. They never tried to duck the "hot ones." With patience and understanding they answered everything as best they could—and their best was of real comfort to me and others.

I have found that you can't tell how religious a man is by what he says, or does.

Before my accident I recall during our combat training that religion never showed much *on* the surface, but was very much there *under* the surface. All of us put up a tough front. We belonged to the school of realism. War was rough, so our actions and talk had to be rough—we figured. And the paratroops, I can safely say, were the toughest bunch of all.

One man in our company, Big Joe, was the most awesome physical specimen I have ever known. Huge in stature, a calloused hulk of muscle, Big Joe swore furiously, drank mightily and was ready to fight at the drop of a hat. He might have been Satan himself as far as the others were concerned, but I knew different.

On our practice jumps I sat next to Big Joe in the plane and jumped right behind him. As the tense moment arrived just before we were to go spilling out into space, I could see Big Joe's face relax. It grew gentle, serene, and his lips moved in a quiet prayer. At this moment I think he felt very close to God. But once on the ground, he was a man of fierce action again, ferocious, grim, the Devil himself.

Not all soldiers concealed their religion with such camouflage. I know of one soldier—we'll call him Steve—who did just the opposite. He was friendly, brimming with good humor, a thorough extrovert in every sense. To appreciate this story, you must get the picture of the inside of an Army barracks. Bunks are lined up on either side, sometimes as many as thirty on one floor. Privacy simply doesn't exist.

In the evening just before lights went out, there was always a terrific hubbub ... men coming in from pass, loud arguing, singing and constant traffic back and forth to the shower. Steve was always right in the middle of the loudest argument or the noisiest singing—until he saw time running short. Then he would break away and hustle out of his clothes.

But just before he climbed into bed, he always knelt quietly with folded hands at the side of his bunk ... *and prayed.*

The noise, the bright lights, the confusion never bothered him.

No one ever made fun of him or kidded him for it. In fact, underneath, these hard-bitten men admired and respected him for his open faith. To them it represented real courage in the face of possible ridicule. But I actually believe that Steve never felt that he was being conspicuous. To him it was the right and natural thing to do.

I mention these few experiences because I have heard so many people say that the youth of today are turning away from religion. Nothing can be farther from the truth. What many people consider irreverence on the part of youth is merely impatience.

Young Americans—especially veterans of the past war—want to see the men of God roll up their sleeves and tackle some problems like these same ex-servicemen tackled the problem, say, of demolishing an enemy pillbox. Just talk isn't enough. They want action!

My chance to act the part of Homer Parrish in *The Best Years of Our Lives* was one of the finest things that will ever happen to me. Not because it made me a Hollywood celebrity, but because it gave me a chance to show thousands of other disabled people that a handicap can give them the necessary impetus to achieve more than if their calamity had never happened.

I know this to be true with many others beside myself. A close friend of mine was a great athlete before he lost both legs. This blow changed the course of his life, and now he is a brilliant lawyer with a great future before him. He admits that but for this accident his present achievements would never have been realized.

There are hundreds, thousands of similar cases. And they were all able to rise from the depths, I feel sure, not only because they had courage, but because they also had a great source of inner power—religious faith.

Illustration, Harold Russell, see page 105

THESE MEN

FOUND

ADVENTURE

PAGE
164

PAGE 1

P

PAGE 159

PAGE 168

PAGE 155

PAGE 141

PAGE 144

PAGE 152

BURIED ALIVE

by EDWARD CHRISTIANSEN

> *A deep sea diver is pinned by tons of mud and cables. Then his diving suit springs a leak . . .*

REPORTERS AND mobile radio units crowded aboard the derrick barge, *Baxter,* one April day back in 1948. Special radio bulletins were being broadcast. I didn't know it, but each time I spoke from the ocean bottom, my words went out over the air.

I was buried alive in my diving suit, under 35 feet of mud and water, off Port Richmond, Staten Island.

"I think this is the end," I called through my phone. "Promise you'll look after my family." Reporters pressed through the crowd to take down the reply of my boss, Captain Sorenson:

"Hold on, Ed. A diver will be here soon. Please hold on."

I was on my back, head down in the mud, knees jackknifed against my chest. The lead weights a diver wears around his waist jammed into my abdomen. My right arm had been caught, flung outward, as if pleading. My left arm was near my chest— a good break because I could control my air valve. The air hose itself was wrapped around my ankle. If the hose kinked, I would suffocate. It was cold in the total blackness.

The accident happened while I was redoing a cable-laying job. Several weeks before, auxiliary telephone cables had been laid at Kill van Kull. But after the job was finished, it was learned they were not down to marine-law requirements of 35 feet below dead-low water. Their depth was 30 feet. That meant they must be put down 5 feet deeper.

To accomplish this, I had to lift the cables and dig a deeper trench with my pressure hose. This created two thick walls of mud, between which the cables had to be laid.

It was not an unusual operation, and after several days' work, my task was nearly completed. I had only ten more feet to go. At nine o'clock, on the 22nd of April, I got into my diving suit and helmet as usual, paused a moment to say a little prayer, and descended. I always pray as I go down, and when I come up I say, "Thank you, God."

I worked for only a short time when suddenly I felt the sweeping shock that sends dread into the soul of the calmest, most experienced diver. The wall of mud was beginning to slide. In a matter of seconds, tons of mud and eighteen four-inch cables fell on top of me.

I could hear just one sound. The precious hiss of air coming into the helmet. But my tough diving mitts had been ripped, and salt water was beginning to seep into my suit.

With the touch of the water came my worst danger—panic! I fumbled for my air hose and twisted it hard. The air rushed in, building pressure up inside my suit, and keeping the water out. But I knew this had increased the danger. Like a tight balloon my suit could tear easily now.

Any diver knows that in an accident fear is his worst enemy. Fear makes for wasting precious strength and courage. It produces spasms.

It is true, the old saying that when a man faces death, he relives, in a few moments, almost his whole life. I thought about my childhood in Oslo, Norway where I was born . . . the death of my parents before I reached the age of seven . . . years of unhappiness with a foster family.

At seventeen, I got a job on a ship which took me to America. In the United States, I met Clara, who became my wife. To support my family (now six children) I became tender to a diver. A tender is the man who lowers and raises the diver, and in those early days, he regulated the air hose, too.

Later I learned to dive myself. In those days, diving was an even more dangerous business than it is today. There were no telephones; the only communication between the diver and tender was the lifeline on which we could communicate by tugging.

Without today's more advanced equipment I would have been dead by the time Captain Frank Sorenson telephoned: "Hold on, Ed, we'll have you free!"

"Has the diver come?" I asked.

I fainted again. How long I was unconscious I've no idea. But I was aroused by a new voice.

"Christiansen—Ed Christiansen!"

"Yes," I breathed.

"I'm from the Navy school. I've brought a crew of ten men to rescue you. Two of the best are going down now."

But suddenly I had a sharp sense that I was going to die. It was the critical moment and I knew it, when death was so close you could almost feel it.

It was then that I asked Captain Sorenson to look after my family. Above all, I told myself, I must keep praying for calm.

And bit by bit, as I contemplated death, a sense of peace settled over me. I lost all fear.

And then I felt myself moving up. "You're okay now," I heard a voice say. I opened my eyes to see the face of my eldest daughter, Elizabeth. "Oh, Daddy," she cried. "I prayed every minute—and God heard me. You're going to be all right."

I had been pinned under four hours. They put me in the decompression chamber to prevent the "bends" and a few hours later they took me out. It wasn't until then I was able to say, with greater meaning than ever before: "Thank you, God."

Illustration, Edward Christiansen, see page 136

STICK PUSHER

by ERNEST W. WEEKS

Come along on a practice jump to learn how a veteran paratrooper handles fear

THE BIG C-119 is ready. You climb up the starboard ladder, walk down the aisle toward the cabin and take the last seat. You're going to be Stick Pusher * again, but who is going to push you out?

At first you're too busy to think. You throw your static line over your right shoulder and sit down; you fumble for your safety belt and stand up to locate it. The bucket seat is uncomfortable; so is the chute and all of your combat equipment.

A voice from the rear says, "After we are airborne, we'll climb to 1200 feet and circle the DZ.** On the first pass we'll give you the green light. You shouldn't have any trouble; we have a six-mile-an-hour ground wind from the northeast away from the bay. You've got twenty men to get out of each door and you've got twelve seconds to do it in. Have a smooth ride. See you on the ground."

The kid next to you is going up for the first time out of school. It's rough on him. He turns to you and asks, "Sarge, are you ever afraid in this business?"

You force a smile and answer seriously, "The guy hasn't been born who isn't afraid when he goes up."

He grins then and says, "Gimme a push if I stop."

You answer automatically, "Don't worry, kid: that's what I'm here for."

Then you start to think.

* The last man to jump, chosen because of his experience.
** Drop zone.

141

"That's the trouble with you: you think too much when you should be trying to relax."

You look at the young frightened faces around you. "Get a hold of yourself, fellow. Think of the younger guys who are looking to you for example. Dear God in Heaven, just give me the calmness and courage to go out that door."

The motors roar louder and the plane begins to lumber slowly down the runway. It picks up speed and you can tell almost the second that the wheels leave the ground.

You try to relax, letting your body go limp all over, but you keep remembering all of the hundreds of little things that could go wrong.

You lift up your mind then and tell the Lord you are in His hands and you don't care what happens to you as long as He helps you go out that door. Yet you can't help but ask, without even forming words, that He spare your life.

Just as your fear begins to subside, a voice shocks you.

"Get ready!"

You take up your static line.

"Stand and hook up!"

You stand up and reach for the anchor line cable.

"Check your equipment!"

You look down at your reserve chute and check the quick release box on your harness, the back pack of the man in front of you and his main lift webs, then your own static line. Then you swing around in the aisle and let the kid check you.

You've been dreading this moment and now it's here. Your heart beats wildly and no clear thoughts are in your mind.

"Get it over with . . . let's get out of here . . . move . . . move . . . move. God give me strength . . . I can't . . ."

Sweat pours from your body and you feel sick and faint. You flex your muscles and are surprised to find them still willing to work.

As you hear the dreaded command to "Go" you find yourself saying, "Yea, though I walk through the valley of the shadow of death, I shall fear no evil . . ."

Before you the men are moving out the door into space. You become fascinated by the bucking of the cable as it receives the pull of the opening chutes.

You move toward the door and suddenly your mind is clear; you see everything that happens in minute detail. The men are going out; you're almost there. Sixteen . . . seventeen . . . eighteen . . . the kid in front of you; and then your heart leaps and you gasp.

Down below you there are chutes in the sky, the kid is hurtling through space with his chute trailing out behind. The ground looks miles away.

You see it all in a split second because you don't stop; you leap up and out into the blast. You only fall free for about two seconds before you're jolted by the shock of your chute's opening, but all that happens to you in those two seconds would make a separate story.

You drift down to the ground, thanking God over and over again. Your heart is filled with the beauty of the world around you; you feel that you are one of the luckiest men alive because you are a paratrooper.

You relax and clobber into the ground. As you get out of your chute, you feel like singing because today you are still a man.

The kid comes up to you. "You're tops, Sarge. Nobody needs to push you."

You can't help but reply, "You're wrong, kid. God's my Stick Pusher."

Illustration, Ernest Weeks, see page 137

WHY WAS I SPARED?

by ARIE BESTEBREURTJE

> *This "cloak-and-dagger" specialist, when dropped behind enemy lines, discovered he had landed inside a concentration camp.*

IT'S BEEN ten years since Jan Schutten, a Netherlands farmer, prevented Nazi soldiers from capturing me—and probably killing me.

Jan, a devoted family man, is now hard at work working his farmland in the village of Hooghalen near Assen. I hope Jan reads this story; in fact, I will dedicate it to him. He, who loved all men as brothers, whose prayer was that men become builders rather than destroyers, would approve a step I've recently taken . . .

Soon after my native Holland was overrun in 1940, I escaped with my wife, Gertrude, to England. There I enlisted in Special Forces, a unit designed for "Cloak and Dagger" work.

Our eight months period of training in the wilds of Scotland was thorough. The emphasis was on destruction. Before breakfast every morning we fired 18 shots with an automatic to master intuitive firing. We learned housebreaking quite scientifically from a "specialist," released from prison for the occasion. We learned about explosives, forgery, and foreign arms. We learned how to tell glib, credible lies and how to kill silently.

Our job was also humanitarian: to rescue pilots shot down in enemy territory and to help political prisoners escape.

Then, one dark night in 1945, four of us from Special Forces took off on a crucial assignment. The final assault on the Netherlands was only a few days off. Our destination was the Westerbork concentration camp in the north of the Netherlands. Our mission: to free the prisoners.

With me were Capt. Robert Harcourt, Lt. C. Ruijsch van Dugteren and Sgt. Somers, a radio operator. Somehow we would have to bribe or bluff the camp commandant into surrendering by convincing him that the Allies would soon overrun the whole countryside. The weather was bad, and we jumped in fog.

I hit hard on the ground. Intense pain gripped my right ankle. Later I found it was broken.

Soon there were shots and barking dogs. German voices shouted orders. Harcourt helped me roll up my parachute and move under a small tree, where he covered me with heather. It was decided I would wait for the others, while Harcourt scouted around.

All night long I waited. And when dawn came, I looked up and saw the enemy flag floating from the top of a building. To the left was a high barbed-wire fence interrupted by watch towers.

I was on the wrong side of the fence and inside the prison camp area I had come to liberate!

True, I was in the outer area, but it was still behind barbed wire. Soon I heard searching parties drawing closer. I had no illusions as to what would happen if I were captured. But the day passed, and I was not discovered. Neither Harcourt nor my other companions showed up that day or night.

Hunger did not bother me as much as thirst. I dug deep into the earth with my hands, scooping out some soupy mud, which I strained through a first-aid bandage and purified with a special tablet. During the mornings I sucked dew from pine needles.

I crawled as close to the fence as I dared. For hours I lay there and studied the guards' habits. Finally, from their gossip, I learned that Harcourt was captured, the others killed and that I was at large.

On the fifth night, weak from hunger, I crawled close to the fence and took out my wire clippers. Holding my breath, I cut the wire and crept through. For one stark moment, the searchlight swept over me, then passed on. No one had noticed.

Painfully, I wormed my way through the countryside for some four miles, then sank exhausted into a ditch where I stayed until daylight. The next day I watched the farmers busy working in the surrounding fields.

When the last one started to leave, I called out to him. But my voice came out a hoarse whisper, like in a bad dream. I had no voice. To get his attention I waved frantically. He saw me. Could I trust him?

"Would you bring me some food and water without telling a soul?" I whispered.

It was a test question. Food was so scarce his family would know if one piece of bread were missing.

"I'll have to ask my father," the youth said. I relaxed a little. This was hopeful. At midnight the boy's father came.

He was Jan Schutten, a stocky man, with big hands and bright, searching eyes. For a few moments we fenced verbally. Soon he satisfied himself I was neither decoy nor spy and admitted he was an underground worker who knew the password and details about our mission. I was hidden in the barn and soon learned that Jan had ten other refugees secreted on the farm.

"Suppose you ran out of food?" I once asked him. Jan looked philosophical.

"God will provide," he answered. He acted as though God were living on the farm with him. "You say the Lord's Prayer, don't you?"

I nodded.

"Well, don't you say, 'Give us this day our daily bread?' Unless you believe it, you shouldn't say it."

It made jolting good sense.

I came to revere this forthright farmer and typical Dutch Protestant, who never missed church, sang loudly the old hymns and was a stickler for grace at mealtime and family Bible reading in the evening. He and his wife took a chance on me, as the Good Samaritan did on the beaten stranger by the roadside.

Nor did Jan concern himself over local German authority and the consequences to him if discovered. He was doing what he felt was right. God was his only Master.

Eventually I made it back to England. A year after the war I came to America and started a business career in New York City, as consultant on European law and affairs. Yet never once did I recall my experiences that I didn't ask myself:

"Did God spare me for a purpose?"

I joined the Huguenot Memorial Church in Pelham, a New York suburb, and became a Sunday school teacher. Later I was promoted to be superintendent in a department, then was elected as an elder of the church. But the memories of my "coincidental" escapes—and the one with Jan was not the only one—did not fade. Nor did I stop asking myself, "Should I not do more to spread the Word? Am I not dodging as Jonah did?"

In war I was taught the destructive techniques. Perhaps they helped win a war, but I also learned that alone we are lost, that whatever we try to achieve can only happen with God's help.

Now I want to spend the rest of my life sharing that conviction.

In the fall of 1953 I enrolled at Union Theological Seminary in New York City. If God will allow me to serve in His ministry, I will do the best I can.

Illustration, Arie Bestebreurtje, see page 137

CRISIS IN
A FORBIDDEN LAND

by **LOWELL THOMAS JR.**

> *A famous team of adventurers explore a little-known land. Then comes the accident—and a rescue down treacherous mountain passes.*

I WAS IN Persia during the early summer of 1949 when this cable arrived from my father:

"The miracle has happened. Permission granted to enter Tibet. Fly to Calcutta and round up supplies. (Signed) Dad."

Tibetans for years had refused to permit visitors into their land of mystery. Now the Dalai Lama and his high priests had thrown open the doors. Why?

We learned later that Tibetans had grown to fear Russia and her obvious yen for Tibet's minerals and route to India, even more than they feared the infiltration of our Western science and culture.

On the last day of July, 1949 my father and I started out from Calcutta with 37 pieces of luggage, bound for Gangtok, capital of Sikkim, where we were to join our mule caravan. There, at the foot of the mighty Himalayas, we picked up 6 baggage-carrying coolies, 9 pack mules and 4 riding ponies. Our caravan also included interpreter, cook and head muleteer—a total of 14.

The really rugged part of the journey was ahead—300 miles along tortuous mountain trails, by sheer precipices, through monsoon rains, to the very roof of the world, Lhasa, capital of Tibet.

Dad, who had dreamed of making a trip to Tibet most of his life, squinted in fascination at the lofty Himalayas. Our interpreter, Tsewong Namgyal, had an uncanny sixth sense. "Kale pe a," he said to my father.

With credit to OUT OF THIS WORLD *by Lowell Thomas Jr. (Greystone Press)*

"What does he mean?" I asked.

"It means—go slowly, if you hope to return," he replied.

Significant, that warning!

We made an average of fifteen miles a day through this fascinating country of 4,000,000 people, most of whom are short, stocky, dark-skinned villagers and nomads. The people of Tibet are Buddhists, theirs being a very spiritual country with deep-rooted religious customs and practices.

Tibetans, for example, are seldom without their 108-bead rosaries. One of the first spiritual symbols we saw were prayer flags. These are bits of cloth which hang from a cord and flutter furiously in the wind. Each time one of these cloths moves, a prayer is wafted to Lord Buddha.

Likewise, prayer wheels or barrels anchored in a rushing stream, are crammed with written prayers. With each revolution of the barrel in the water, all prayers inside are repeated again and again to mighty Buddha.

Tibetans believe in reincarnation. The purer your life, the higher form it will take when reborn, possibly even a government official or an incarnate lama. Sinners go down the ladder, however, and may end up as animals, according to Buddhist doctrine.

The prestige and authority of the high priests are enormous. Nearly one-fourth of all Tibetans enter the priesthood, while monasteries cover the whole country. Discipline is rigid.

We made the trip to Lhasa without mishap, where we were received with great hospitality by the Dalai Lama and his high officials. They cooperated with our every wish, whether it be to make transcriptions of festivals, take pictures of all the high chieftains, or visit the most sacred sanctuaries. Only too soon did we have to begin our return jaunt down the same perilous passes which we had climbed.

During our fifth day of descent I was in the lead when

suddenly I heard a commotion behind. Turning, I was just in time to see Pop sail through the air from his horse and land hard on the sharp rocks.

Dad, barely able to move, struggled to keep consciousness. Accidents at high altitude can mean quick death, and a man with a weaker heart could never have withstood the shock. Since we had no doctor and our first aid kit was miles behind with the supply caravan, I sent our interpreter galloping to the nearest village to round up porters to help us carry him in.

That first night was a nightmare for Pop. Sleep was impossible because of a high fever. Thank God for his top physical condition and self-discipline, developed during a life-time of world travel.

The only doctor we knew of was miles away at a town called Gyantse. Only through an antiquated telephone, with wires that blew down whenever a high wind or storm occurred, could we reach him. We could apply first aid, yet without a doctor for professional advice in splinting Dad's leg. I couldn't see how we would ever get him home.

But prayer was answered—we were able to contact the doctor, who arrived by forced march. He examined the patient, then explained that while surgery was not his field, he felt it was only a muscular injury. Actually, without an X-ray, there was no way to tell that the femur was cracked in eight places. So we decided to continue our journey.

It sometimes took 10 Tibetans to carry the stretcher over the steep rocky trails, which skirted chasms and swift streams. Strapped to his stretcher, with his leg in a splint, Dad roasted under the sun and nearly froze when clouds and cold winds blotted it out.

Meanwhile we explored every possibility of speeding him home. Flying was out—no airfields, plus the fact that planes were forbidden to fly over Tibet. When he could sit up, we fashioned a stout wooden sedan chair, with tarpaulin over the top, to keep Pop out of the elements.

Tibetans in teams of four would carry this sedan chair. The prayer chant they sang as they plodded along still drums through our brains. Translated it was: "Oh Lord Buddha, lighten our load!" Over and over they sang it, with occasional awed glances at the nearby sacred Tibetan mountain of Chamalhari, 24,000 feet high.

I marvelled at the way Dad kept his sense of humor despite the continual bounce of his wooden litter. Several times he tried to teach his bearers new songs. At other times he chanted with them. And at night, in his fitful sleep, he mumbled right in tune: "Oh Lord Buddha, lighten our load!"

Then, on the fifth of October we were met by a rescue team sent out by Loy Henderson, U. S. Ambassador at New Delhi, India. What a gorgeous sight it was! Then we flew halfway around the world to America in the same length of time it took to hike 40 tortuous miles in the land of the Lamas.

The trip officially ended with our delivery to President Truman of the Dalai Lama's message, handwritten in Tibetan characters with a bamboo pen on parchment made from the bark of a Tibetan tree:

" . . . *We, the government and people of Tibet, are much worried and deeply concerned over the present state of the world in which we live. And we are eager to have it known that here in Tibet, a land that is especially dedicated to religion, all of our peoples, both lay and monk, are earnestly praying that God will grant happiness and everlasting peace to all humanity."*

I've thought about that message and our own test of faith quite a bit since returning from Tibet. Both my father and I are very grateful, if, in any way, we have helped build a bridge of understanding between this land of Buddhism and our own.

Illustration, Lowell Thomas Jr., see page 136

ONE SECOND
FROM ETERNITY

by EDWIN BERRY

Blown out of his jet over the Alaskan wastes, this flyer had a one-in-a-million chance.

It STARTED back in 1950 when I received military orders recalling me to service with the Air Force. Along with hundreds of veterans on reserve status. I was hastily indoctrinated, given a flight physical, and assigned to duty as a radar observer. Seated behind my pilot, in a swift all-weather jet fighter, it would be my job to operate an "electronic eye" and search out invisible enemy aircraft in the darkness.

On December 13th, 1950 I was at Ladd Air Force Base near Fairbanks, Alaska. With my pilot, Capt. Glenn Jackson, we flew patrol missions over the vast square miles of Alaska tundra.

As a World War II flier, I can recall being sustained by the philosophy I got from reading "God is My Co-Pilot" by Robert Lee Scott. The author's faith in God gave him an almost buoyant attitude which helped him survive dangerous air attacks and a crash into hostile country. Almost all fliers develop a strong philosophy of some kind. I didn't realize how much I was to need mine—and how soon.

The temperature was well below zero one day as we whistled down the runway in early afternoon at the start of one mission. The sky was steel-grey and menacing, as is usual in the Arctic winter. Otherwise all was as it should be, with our F-94 jet fighter humming smoothly as we lifted to altitude.

On course, we were directed by the Ground Control Intercept station at Fairbanks, whose powerful radar kept our position known through the entire flight. Our air speed was in excess of

400 miles per hour, while I scanned the empty sky through the invisible fingers of my radar set.

Then, some 30 miles from the base, there was a shattering explosion of sound. I was slammed back in my seat by an icy blast of air, which tore loose the heavy plastic canopy overhead. It vanished in the mists behind. With it went my helmet, containing my earphones and oxygen mask. My eyes were blinded by the freezing slipstream. Since I could not live long in the refrigerated atmosphere with its thin oxygen, there seemed no choice but to bail out.

Facing me were two tremendous obstacles. One was the heavy radar indicator, the size of a large suitcase, which fitted down tightly over my lap from its hinges at the front of the cockpit. The other was the lack of an explosive ejection seat, the type which catapults the jet flier up 50 feet, free of the aircraft. I could force myself over the side, but feared I would be dashed against the rudder or other tail services.

In a spot like this you turn everything over to the Almighty, and all your actions are a prayer.

I tried to push the radar indicator from my lap to its vertical position. With my cockpit wide open, I found myself pushing the indicator forward inch by inch against a 400 mile per hour blast. Then it locked and I was free to crawl up over the side.

As I forced myself blindly out into the slipstream, I felt my hair literally tearing out by the roots. When my foot braced against a solid surface, I catapulted myself into the air.

Instantly there was an impact and a wave of pain, as I struck the stabilizer, projecting up at the tail. After this moment of quick agony, there was only numbness.

My unconscious body plummeted toward the frozen earth thousands of feet below. I have no remembrance of that extended free fall, nor how far I dropped. I only know that as I approached 1000 feet above the ground, something brought me feebly back to consciousness. It took seconds before I realized that I was plunging through the sky, and more seconds to clutch the rip-cord of my parachute. It opened with a soft report, tugged at me only once, then I plowed into a deep snowbank.

The snowbank, encrusted with rime ice in the subzero cold, broke my fall for the most part. Dimly conscious I saw the parachute flutter out in a semicircle about me, and was grateful that its great colorful stripes would be visible from miles away if a search plane should come this way.

As I lay almost completely buried in the dry, powdery snow, I could scarcely move, and through the semi-coma which enveloped me, I knew that bones were broken and that blood was seeping down my neck. The same prayer consciousness that started with the accident still surrounded me.

As I lay in developing lassitude, with a pleasant torpor stealing over me, I heard the whirring beat of helicopter wings. Numbly I moved my head around to see an Air Rescue Service "eggbeater" hovering overhead cautiously, then swoop to earth a few yards away.

In minutes I was lifted onto a stretcher, covered warmly, and flown to the base hospital. A flight of F-94's had gone on search immediately after news of our mishap, and spotted my parachute. With machinelike efficiency my approximate position had been plotted, and the helicopter crew located me.

My pilot, incidentally, had not lost his helmet and earphones when the canopy was torn away. As a result he was still in radio contact with the field and was able to maneuver down to the runway for a successful landing. Not until the aircraft had rolled to a stop did he realize that I had bailed out.

It required several months to effect my recovery. Some may say I was just lucky. But luck didn't give me the strength I needed when it really counted.

Illustration, Edwin Berry in jet fighter, see page 137

FIND YOUR OWN FRONTIER

by HARRY MORGAN

*Here's a young man who shows how it's possible to
be a Daniel Boone today.*

IT ALL STARTED back in high school. One of my classmates com-
plained that the age of Daniel Boone had passed, and with it
the challenge of new frontiers. I disagreed, and set about looking for an opportunity to prove him wrong.

Through one of my teachers at the Salinas High School, I
learned about the United Nations Institute Workshop* in Montclair, New Jersey. I hitch-hiked there, attended the 1951 summer session on a scholarship, and found my pioneering spirit
excited by the challenge facing the world today in the field of
international relations.

By the time I had returned home to California in September,
I was fired with an ambition to help save the world.

Throughout that winter I helped organize 100,000 high school
students into a United Nations study group. Graduating the following June, I again attended the Montclair Institute and then
went on to the Colgate University summer conference on foreign
policy. I paid my expenses by ushering and working in dining
rooms.

When I got back to Salinas, in the fall, I worked the sugar
beet harvest to bolster my college fund and, that winter, called
on my draft board. Their advice was not to start college—that
I probably had only six months before my call would come.
Should I enlist, I wondered, or was there something constructive, toward my new pioneering goal, that I could do with those
six months?

* *Annual, two-week seminar sponsored by State Teacher's College of Upper
Montclair.*

Over and over I had heard it stressed that the foundation of brotherly love, which had to be the corner stone for world peace, could only come if I *met* my brother. Through our church fellowship, which emphasizes Jesus' teachings, I learned that to work with, or for another, made him your brother. But, where could I work, and for whom?

Then, in February of '53, I read of the great devastating floods sweeping the Netherlands. Since I had been friendly with a lad from Amsterdam named Gerhard Bedding, I decided to do something about helping Gerhard and his friends.

I started East, thumbing my way. In Chicago I stopped for the Welcome Traveler radio show because I knew they served breakfast. Learning of my destination, they gave me a free air ticket from New York to Holland. I hurried on to New York.

At the Netherland Relief Headquarters I asked where I could serve best. "Oh, they don't need workers," a lady said coolly. "They need funds."

But I hadn't any funds to give. Only myself. So I boarded the trans-Atlantic, K.L.M. plane, anyhow, on a chance she was wrong.

In a few hours I was in Holland, ready for what I hoped would be colorful, spectacular rescue work. Only it didn't work exactly that way. My friend Gerhard advised me to join a Quaker work party, and so, with some others, I went to S. Gravendeel, a small village south of Rotterdam.

The villagers laughed when they first saw us, with our clean overalls and new shovels. And they wouldn't trust us to clean their homes, either.

Instead we were permitted to clean the streets, deep under muck and ooze, dead animal life, garbage, and debris that had once been household treasures. It was back-breaking, monotonous work.

I began to find out what *I* was made of. It wasn't nearly strong enough to save the world. Every day I was ready to leave, but every night, as we gathered together, one of our group would tell me I hadn't *given* enough, yet, to gain any understanding of the peoples we were trying to serve. Then we'd sing, and pray, and discuss the example of Christ. Much to my surprise, I'd be built up for the next day's work.

When our job was done the burgomeister called us together and said thanks, haltingly. He handed each of us a small box and inside we found a little silver spoon with a picture of the village in the bowl. It made me ashamed of the mental arithmetic I had been doing on what two weeks shovel work should be worth, by the hour.

Next we went to Dreischor on Schouwen-Duiveland. The town was built in a circle around a lovely old 14th century church now coated with mud three inches thick. Half of us began clearing the church while the others tackled the school house. The space was needed to store Red Cross supplies.

Then the people began drifting back, silent and stricken. Most of them had lost so much they didn't know whether to leave forever or to try and salvage what was left. We were waiting to clean homes, but no one called on us. We sensed they distrusted us.

Finally one young couple asked our help. In we went with shovels, brooms, buckets, and cleared the worst of the mess. When we finished our leader shook his head.

"Start all over," he said. "Clean it *completely,* now, so they can resume living. Try to understand. They have no hope. We must give it to them."

That took three more days. When the young family came to look, suddenly we saw smiles for the first time. Again some bands around my heart burst.

Up and down the street ran the young couple dragging friends and relatives to see the miracle wrought in their home. Little by little more homes invited us to come in with our shovels and buckets. As we continued working I began to realize why it wasn't enough just to work for free, we had to work also with understanding and love.

Once again our job was done and we found ourselves in the Town Hall, facing the burgomeister. He knelt before a huge iron safe, removed a box, and distributed "small tokens to express our big thanks." They were teaspoons, with a picture of the town in the bowl. This time there was something in my throat I couldn't seem to swallow.

Before I came home, a Dutch family of small means insisted on sharing with me the vacation tour they had been planning ever since they left a concentration camp. So together we saw the real Europe, as seen by the people who live there.

I returned to America with seven dollars and two teaspoons. But no beaver skins brought back by Daniel Boone were ever more highly valued. To me they are the symbol of an unmeasurable treasure that "moths could not corrupt."

I can honestly say to any young American, "You *can* be a pioneer, today, in the biggest adventure of your life . . . a challenging frontier stretches across our world . . . daring persons are needed there, to bring His Kingdom each day a little nearer, through *active* brotherly love.

Illustration, Harry Morgan, see page 137

ON GETTING TO THE TOP

by MAYNARD MILLER

> *No American had ever climbed the "Saint". This is the account of a tough, treacherous expedition with hair-raising escapes made possible only by "guts" and miracles of team-work.*

COME WITH ME on a mountain climb—with an expedition which took three years to organize and eight weeks to accomplish.

Come with me in spirit and see if you can sense what I mean when I say that veteran mountain climbers, for the most part, are truly spiritual persons. After pitting their strength against the toughest obstacles in the world, they not only find reward in adventure, but also deep communion with God and a cleansing of mind, body, and spirit.

A climb can develop new qualities in one, for the struggle to reach the top is motivated by much more than egotistic ambition. It holds hope and engenders faith. It helps one meet the struggle of life itself with new vision and purpose.

Disappointing as it is sometimes for an expedition to fail in reaching its goal, achievement does not always mean climbing to the top. Satisfaction lies in coping with the problems of a climb intelligently and safely. The attempt alone can give all a sharper perspective on life, teach teamwork, and bring about a better understanding of human nature. And failure is usually only a postponement until the next try.

We faced a mighty tough adversary back in 1946 when eight of us, under the flag of the Harvard Mountaineering Club, prepared to climb eighteen-thousand-foot Mount St. Elias. No American had ever stood on the summit of the "Saint," as we familiarly dubbed this great mountain, fourth highest peak in

North America, and the mightiest marker post on the Alaskan-Yukon border.

It wasn't just a "climbing trip"—we had to lug all kinds of extra equipment, and what we couldn't carry had to be parachuted by aircraft. Geological and weather studies were to be made, as well as many special equipment and physiological tests, among which was the "step test" for the analysis of pulse rate at high altitudes. We kept records of water consumption, of hunger, and fatigue. It was genuine research, and real adventure.

During the course of this adventure we became steadily aware that the challenge and test of our mountain was symbolic of life itself, a stimulating blend of "hard and easy going" and of disappointment and success.

The "Saint," we knew, would be ever alert to catch us off balance; it would throw across our path yawning crevasses, rumbling avalanches, and treacherous ice slicks.

A tremendous coastal glacier interposed the first tough barrier. Laden with ninety-pound packs, we had to zig-zag, cut corners, and cross narrow crevasses by snow bridges. When the sun shone on windless days, temperature reached as high as eighty-five degrees. An untaped nose quickly became scorched and red. If we shed shirts, severe sunburn followed. There was a good excuse to let beards grow. If we shaved, sunlight reflected from the snow would soon have seared the undersides of our chins.

A mountain expedition moves by a series of shuttling operations that are carried on between permanent or semi-permanent camps established on ridge tops and on the safe side of slopes. After days of glacier travel, we reached Camp 7 at the base of the main mountain mass. Here we held a "seventh-inning stretch." Strains of harmonica playing, swelling and ebbing across the lonely subarctic land, lulled and relaxed us before the actual "attack" on the peak was to begin.

This camp was in an unexpected heather meadow, a veritable

flowery dell surrounded by formidable rock cliffs and vast stretches of ice. It caused one of the party, Ben Ferris, to express the momentary sentiment: "Let's stay here for the rest of the summer. To heck with going any higher."

Next morning, however, we eagerly looked ahead up the chosen route and saw the sinuous glaciated rim of a hug cirque, or ice-floored amphitheater, twisting upwards for miles toward the top. Several of us pioneered along the avalanche-swept cliffs that walled the cirque.

I was the last man on the rope, having just climbed out of a steep gully. There was only split-second warning—the ominous *swish* that always precedes the breaking away of an avalanche. No sound is more frightening; to be in the path of an avalanche is like facing a thousand trucks thundering along wheel to wheel.

Looking up, I saw a huge swirling mass of ice and snow pouring toward us. Then it thundered past not ten feet away, where we had been but a few moments before. Tons of broken ice, snow, and rock boiled by and out into space, spewing onto the glacier flats below.

Close! I breathed a prayer of thanks.

A relatively easier stretch above this point allowed us to regain our composure, and permitted us to reach the 10,400-foot level before nightfall. Here we established camp on the very crest of a spectacular snow-corniced ridge. There was a tranquillity and a peace of mind, a "refreshment of spirit," inspired by the flushed rose sunset glow reflected from the alpine snows.

But the next morning we awoke to a disappointing contrast. We could hear a dry and ominous puttering at the walls of the tent—freshly falling snow. For seven days we were marooned by the blizzard in that tiny close-packed tent, sickened by the odor of stove gasoline, discomforted by damp clothing—tired, frustrated men practicing every ounce of patience known.

When the storm passed, we carefully studied the route of the last steps which we would have to make. To reach the sharp pyramidal summit of the "Saint" would require two more camps. Camp 10 was next established at 13,400 feet. Here it was time again for the U. S. Air Force support plane to drop us precious food supplies, which it had been doing regularly at intervals all the way up the mountain.

Then I did a very foolish thing! I unroped myself, took a camera and stepped back a few feet from one of the tent pits to get both camp and approaching plane into the picture.

Without warning, I felt myself drop. Instinctively, I spread my arms. By sheer luck, they held on the edges of the hole, abruptly stopping my fall.

I don't think I breathed again until a couple of the boys ran over and pulled me out. Peering into the abyss that had almost swallowed me, I couldn't see botton. It apparently was part of a buried crevasse behind the cornice overhanging the eight thousand-foot cliff in front of our camp. I had learned a lesson in mountain safety which I will never forget—how disastrous it could be to be caught off guard.

To make matters worse, the two big boxes of supplies from the plane missed the target area and smashed to bits on a glacier far below, where I had come so close to falling. It wasn't the pilot's fault, as the weather was rapidly turning sour. We would have to race both weather and our dwindling supplies to reach the top.

Now we were climbing almost entirely over difficult rock and ice. Crampons (two-inch spikes which fasten over climbing boots) were an absolute necessity. Three men were put on a 120-foot rope, so that if one slipped the other two could dig in and hold him until he regained his footing. Teamwork was vital, with everyone adjusting to the slowest person. There are people in life who whine because they feel that someone else is holding them back. None of that with veteran climbers. I wish the whiners could be a part of a climb and feel the vitality that comes from everyone striving for a common goal.

After setting up Camp 11 at 15,500 feet, we were ready for the final effort. The next morning, in the penetrating cold of sub-zero temperature, we were off early. Altitude began to tell on our progress. Wind, whipping powdered snow, and constant searching for secure footholds were exhausting. We climbed upward for ten wearisome hours, higher and higher, from terrace to terrace. "How much longer?" we kept asking ourselves.

Suddenly Dee Molenaar, the front man, let loose with his familiar yodel, "Five feet more of slack and I'll be on top."

Fatigue, headaches, pounding hearts, and all queries as to the state of our sanity were quickly forgotten as we crawled up the final feet of the narrow and ice-armored ridge. Then that stimulating sense of exultation and triumph. We felt like the most important persons on earth.

And yet, paradoxically, at the same time we felt a great humility and an utter insignificance in the apparent vastness of nature's scheme. Everywhere below us rocky glacier-hung domes and spires jutted up through the sea of clouds. Eternity stretched in every direction. How could any man look upon such a spectacle and doubt the existence of God?

We had no wonder why the poet of the Psalms wrote long ago: "I will lift up mine eyes unto the hills from whence cometh my help." We knew that strength and power come from above, and it was easy to understand why Christ's greatest visions and most powerful teachings were delivered on a mountaintop.

Illustration, Maynard Miller and mountain companion, see page 137

CAPTAIN VIDEO'S
TOUGHEST MISSION

by **AL HODGE**

*In this make-believe drama, Al Hodge, who plays
the TV role of Captain Video, plunges through
space, combating evil in the world of the year 3,000
A.D. On weekends, his battle changes only its dress
as he takes over as Sunday School superintendent
for the Manhasset, Long Island, Congregational
Church. There, Hodge emphasizes the role his
seventh and eighth graders can play as Junior Video
Rangers.*

SUDDENLY, in the control tower of my secret mountain headquarters, not far from Planet City, I heard the mechaniphone
buzz. The message was from Charles Carey, Commissioner of
Public Safety:

*"Signal Red. Signal Red. Fear monstrous plot. Sixth church
bombed . . . Synagogues burned . . . Evil space force suspected.
Come immediately."*

Within minutes I was in Planet City, pressing my way through
angry, milling crowds. Commissioner Carey met me at the Capitol steps: "Video, we've called an emergency meeting of The
Solar Alliance. Want you to sit in. Very dangerous. We're afraid
someone has discovered a *hate ray.*"

"Hate ray?" I asked.

The Commissioner lowered his voice, "Not so loud. We don't
want any more rumors than we've got."

A special armed guard rushed us through the crowd past the
Universal Court, where one of our top officials was delivering
a summary so astounding I could not believe my ears.

"This decision is, therefore, handed down against you, not

because of the justice in the case, but because you belong to a religion which I cannot tolerate."

"See what I mean, Captain?" the Commissioner said as we entered the meeting of Solar Alliance officials.

"Ah, Video," a man in uniform said, crisply. "We won't waste time with formalities. Your job is clear. You must discover what is building up this hatred. If there is such a monstrous thing as a hate ray, destroy it."

"We have only one clue," another said. "Count Callisto has escaped from Space Penitentiary. He's smart enough to realize that if he can destroy our religions, he can control the universe."

I contacted my Rangers at strategic points about the world, told them to take bearings on any unknown rays. We worked desperately.

"Agents 36 and 42 reporting. Six degrees solar deviation from moon." Later: "H-R reporting. Asimometer calculation indicates moon . . ."

I signaled the control tower to fuel up our space ship, X-9, for a trip to the moon. Aboard, I briefed the crew about Callisto's escape and the hate ray. My good friend, Ranger, asked me, "Why's he after the churches, Captain?"

"They're our greatest strength, Ranger. Callisto knows it. First he destroys the churches. Then it'll be race again race, planet against planet. It'll mean *fear* in the universe again. Greed. Selfishness. War. That's how he can run things."

But, as we approached the bright side of the moon, Ranger became sultry and silent until suddenly he turned on me: "Video, you're all wet about this church business. You belong to the wrong church yourself."

I started to snap back, feeling a strange tug of hate, then stopped. "The hate rays!" I shouted. "Struggle against them, men. If we fall here . . . no chance of saving Planet City from Callisto." And immediately, as if in answer to my speech, there came over our audiophone a low chuckling.

"Ha, ha, ha. Hello, suckers. This is Callisto calling. Hating each other just a little? That's just the first step . . . "

I realized that Callisto must have a neutralizer for the deadly rays; otherwise hate would destroy his own crew. Sending X-9 ahead as a decoy, I quietly boarded my space jeep, shot around the dark side of the moon. The effect of Callisto's hate ray was still strong.

I had to operate entirely by radar, feeling my way through the crags and pits of the moon's surface. Then, ahead of me, shooting out into space, I could see a faint glimmer of light.

Cutting off my rocket, I glided quietly in and dismounted. I could see that there were no guards present. Callisto had been overconfident. A few yards away was a weird apparatus, something like an electroscope antenna. This must certainly be the neutralizer station. It was aimed at a nearby mountain peak, where Callisto's headquarters must be located. He would have a large crew there, and I was alone.

Then I discovered a strange thing. I didn't want to step into the neutralizing rays. My instinct was to keep my hate. This was why Callisto's weapon was so deadly . . . hate destroys us from within; we don't *want* to follow the principal of "Love your enemies." It took sheer will-power to force myself into the area of the rays. I could feel a great healing warmth, instead of hate, taking over again in my own soul. I felt invigorated and saw instantly what I must do.

I swung the neutralizing rays away from Callisto's headquarters into the direction of our ship, the X-9.

The results were immediate. Out of Callisto's headquarters swarmed struggling, fighting, quarreling men. Naturally, the hate rays were especially effective against men who had not built up a resistance through love. Callistro, himself, followed, bewildered and stunned.

"Quick, men! To the neutralizer," he shouted.

But they never made it. For a moment Callisto's strong personality rallied his men. They started in my direction, but before they had come a hundred yards they were quarreling and confused again.

I signalled X-9 to come quickly to the neutralizer. From our stations, we watched as Callisto's power was broken by his own hate rays. Twenty minutes later, it was a simple matter to round up the entire mob.

After destroying the ray, we brought Callisto back to Earth, where he is now resting safe and sound in Space Penitentiary. The designs were discovered in Callisto's headquarters. Commissioner Carey and myself are the only others who have ever seen them. One cold winter afternoon, we burned the designs in Carey's fireplace.

"Well, Captain," he said, "thanks to you and your men, we have this again . . ."

He opened the window. From the door of a nearby church came the laughs and singing of the kids in a Sunday School class in Planet City; as they worked together helping the workmen rebuild their church.

Illustration, Al Hodge, see page 136

A DOOLITTLE BOY
GOES BACK

by **JACOB DeSHAZER**

When Jimmy Doolittle arrived in Japan, during the time of the recent Korean conflict, he said: "There is just one man whom I particularly want to see—Jacob DeShazer." Here is why.

IT IS HARD to describe the feeling I had back in 1948 as I stood on shipboard heading for Japan—the same destination as six years before. This mission—brotherhood; a far different objective than the one I had back in 1942.

I thought back to my youth and our home in the wheat-growing section of Madras, Oregon. Here my mother and step-father had brought me up on prayer and Bible reading.

In high school I turned away from my early training, quarreled frequently with my parents, and lived as I pleased. My crowd scoffed at the Church and religion. But the pleasures to which I devoted myself never fully satisfied me.

The Army Air Corps answered my craving for adventure. I won my wings as a bombardier shortly before the war. Soon afterward came the offer of a dangerous mission, one of these yes-or-no propositions. I said "Yes." When we learned that Jimmy Doolittle was to be our chief, our pulses really quickened.

A hint as to the whereabouts of our mission came when we were told that neither the Norden bombing sight nor radio equipment would be used. They were afraid of capture! Then for many weeks we were put under a most intense training period.

One day we flew to the Coast, where we saw the aircraft carrier *Hornet* docked. Later I saw the claws of a tremendous crane reach down and swing up our plane unto the deck of that ship.

On April 18, 1942, just eight hundred miles from Japan we were alerted for the final take-off from the carrier deck of the *Hornet*. The waves were tremendous. Our plane and crew of five was the sixteenth and last to take off.

When we reached the Japanese coast, we dropped our four bombs.

Later, when our gas supply was virtually exhausted, our whole crew bailed out over the central part of China. I landed on a grave, but the ground beneath me felt so good that I found myself hugging the gravestone.

Then a group of soldiers, who claimed to be Chinese, intercepted us. They were Japs. We were beaten, tortured, and made to sit through a mock trial. The Japanese judge spoke only his own language, and we had no interpreter. After this farce, three of our group were taken out and shot, and the remaining men were sentenced to life imprisonment. My hatred for these people knew no bounds and I was sustained only in the thought of eventual revenge.

We were imprisoned for forty months, only 170 days of which were not in solitary confinement. My antagonism almost ate away my reason. Guards kicked us, prodded us, even hit us over the heads with their scabbards. Lieutenant Meder of our group became sick and died.

After that, the treatment became slightly better. One day Captain Kato, one of the top authorities, issued a book to each of us. *It was the Bible!* God must have prompted this amazing action.

As I began to leaf through, my thoughts wandered back to my youth, and the family prayer and Scripture readings we used to have. Eagerly I bent over these pages again. When I had finished, something had changed inside me. The bitterness was gone. The prospect of eternal life suddenly became real to me, and I was determined to keep Christ's commandments.

For a long time I pondered: *A new commandment I give unto*

you, That ye love one another; as I have loved you. (John 13:34)

There was no compromising with this passage. Christ didn't mean to love only those who were on your side. He meant to love both friends and enemies. I realized that the greatest possible weapon in the hands of men is love. With it wars would be impossible.

With every bit of humility I could summon, I prayed to God that He would forgive me as I wanted to forgive the Japs. Gradually the feeling grew that it wasn't enough just to forgive. God wanted me to come back to Japan with the Gospel instead of bombs.

When the war ended, we were released from prison on August 20, 1945. After nearly a four-year absence, it is little wonder that our reception in America nearly steered me off the track. But I was determined to return to Japan as a missionary. First I had to go to school. I am convinced that God directed me to the Seattle Pacific College where I met Florence Matheny, a girl from Toddville, Iowa, who became my wife.

We graduated from school together, received our B.A. degrees, and were appointed as missionary candidates to go to Japan under the auspices of the General Missionary Board of the Free Methodist Church of North America at Winona Lake, Indiana.

On December 14, 1948, my wife and I, with our little son, sailed out from the San Francisco harbor on the U. S. S. *General Meigs.*

How would we be received? Could a people so thoroughly devastated by air bombardment as the Japanese extend the open hand of friendship to one who had taken part in this destruction?

No sooner had we disembarked on Japanese soil than the calls deluged us. They came from all over Japan.

But the star attraction was not "the Doolittle flyer," nor a group of Americans with candy bars—it was Jesus Christ and

His message. The hunger for religion in Japan is overwhelming.

Many greeted us with little enthusiasm, in some cases open hostility. One girl, in particular, watched me so constantly that she began to make me self-conscious.

"Can I help you in some way?" I asked. She hurried away, but something in her eyes had chilled me. I recognized bitter hatred.

During one of our next meetings, which she attended, I emphasized how Jesus can change hatred to love. Then I told of my prison experience.

The change in this one girl was startling. In a few weeks she became one of the most enthusiastic of the group. My wife and I frequently held informal home discussions and she came on several occasions. Then one night she finally confessed that she had been determined to kill me. Her sweetheart was killed during the war, and she had sworn vengeance against the newly arrived American flyer. It was an act of God that the girl attended that one particular meeting on love. The message worked the same change inside her it had in me in the Japanese prison camp.

But the high point of our activity occurred recently in a big theater in Osaka. All of the Japanese prison guards who could be found, many who had treated us with cruelty as our captors, were invited to a gathering in this theater. About two thousand people were on hand, including my former guard, Captain Kato.

Out of this meeting came a demonstration of the teaching which Jesus gave—and which had changed my whole life— "Love your enemies." As a result of the services some of the guards expressed a desire to become Christians.

I could hardly say "mission accomplished" yet. But a start has been made. We are adding our bit to what hundreds of other missionaries are doing around the world.

Illustration, Jacob DeShazer, holding son, see page 137

EXTRAORDINARY

PROJECTS

OF ORDINARY

YOUTH

GE 190

PAGE 174

PAGE
180

PAGE 195

PAGE
183

THE MODERN PIED PIPER

by **LEN LeSOURD**

*Choir kids build a $35,000 pipe organ! "Ridiculous,"
said their parents. But a famous radio commentator
didn't think so. An amazing story of perseverance.*

DINNER was over. Fulton Lewis, Jr. arose from the table and
started to his study for a long evening of work on a special broadcast—a task already postponed too many times.

"Tonight," the broadcaster announced with that determined
look his family knew so well . . . "Tonight I'm not to be disturbed *for anything—not even for St. Peter himself.*"

Once in his study, he closed the door firmly and settled himself at his desk. But his mind still rang with the shouts of some
thirty harum-scarum youngsters whom, as their choirmaster,
he had gathered together that afternoon and conducted on a
60-mile trip to Washington, D.C. for singing instruction.

Outside he heard the doorbell ring. Rigidly he tried to concentrate on the papers before him, but the sound of youthful
voices talking to his wife filtered through.

"Say, we've got something really important to ask Mr. Lewis."

"I'm very sorry, but he just can't be disturbed."

Fulton Lewis sighed, laid down his pen and went out.

"Okey, Kids," the broadcaster said dryly, "what's so important?"

15-year-old Bobby Adams, son of a local bricklayer, spoke up.

"None of us ever heard anything as beautiful as that pipe
organ today. We decided to chip in and buy one for our church.
How do we go about it?"

"Do you know how much a pipe organ costs?" Lewis asked
quizzically.

"As much as $500?"

"About $25,000—for a small one."

The youngsters looked stunned.

"If you want a pipe organ bad enough," said Lewis, "you'll have to go out and build one yourselves. Goodnight, kids."

Back at his desk, Lewis squirmed uncomfortably in his chair. "How did I get myself in for all this?"

"All this" referred to the local children and their choir project which music-lover Lewis had taken on months before. It started when many of his neighbors, disturbed by the spiritual drought throughout St. Mary's County, banded together and built a Methodist church outside of the little town of Hollywood, Maryland. Fulton Lewis, Jr., who lived with his family two miles away at Placid Harbor, helped dedicate the sanctuary on his 1947 Christmas Eve broadcast. As a last minute idea, he gathered together a small group of kids for a junior choir.

This new church was a healthy spot in an area peppered with more bars than grocery stores, more gambling joints than churches and many more poor than well-to-do. Youngsters from these families were in the group that approached Fulton Lewis, Jr., several days after the broadcast to ask him to be regular choirmaster for their planned junior choir.

Something in their faces grabbed his heart as they came timidly before him with their proposition. His own youngsters, Betsy, 17, and Buddy, 14, had also been working on him. Sure—he'd be glad to train them, but they would have to work hard.

Who would have imagined that these untrained and often untalented youngsters, ranging from 9 to 17 years, would through persistence, patience and practice, quickly learn some 200 hymns by heart, take to four-part harmony and become a disciplined, imaginative singing body?

But now for his broadcast . . . As he started back to his desk, the doorbell rang again.

"Mr. Lewis," blurted Bobby Adams, "we decided we can build a pipe organ. But we need your help—just like with the choir."

Lewis looked over the youngsters' eager faces. "When we started this choir, I stated that if you had faith in yourselves, you could work miracles," he said. "You have with the choir. But building a pipe organ is a fantastically intricate job. If you'll work twice as hard, though, we'll tackle it."

Would they!

"Remember this, though . . . No outside professional help. We do the job ourselves—or it doesn't get done. Okey?"

"Okey!"

On the morning of May 17, 1948, villagers along Maryland Highway 235 witnessed an unusual sight. A truck hove into view, piled high with an assortment of pipes. Fulton Lewis, Jr., at the wheel of the truck, pulled in front of the community church and 700 pipes were quickly disgorged over the church lawn. Kids soon swarmed in from every direction, armed with brushes, buckets of water and glass wax. Overhead the warm rays of a May sun poured down on the scrubbing party as the youngsters bathed and polished pipes, handling delicate parts with a tenderness usually reserved for a precious possession. Local people had never seen anything like it.

Late in the day, grunting, sweating youths reloaded the pipes into a truck for transfer to the Lewis basement. Mrs. Lewis saw at once that her days of orderly housekeeping were over. Her home soon resembled a tool shop as boxes of parts, wires, connections and lumber began to pile up. And pipes everywhere!

Meanwhile, every spare minute, Fulton Lewis pored over a little volume on the technique of organ construction.

Every youngster pitched in. Nothing glamorous about sandpapering the same pipes over and over again . . . or cutting leather diaphragms for the hundreds of needed pneumatics until hands were cramped and aching . . . or twisting wires around contact pins until fingers were raw. The total of 15,000 needed electrical connections seemed staggering.

Mrs. Lewis, resigned to her home becoming a recreational hall, set up her own school—for manners. It wasn't unusual to hear her kind but firm voice lining them up in fives and sixes and instructing them in the art of meeting new people, and introducing each other to strangers. Dedication to their choir and pipe organ projects gave the youngsters a new sense of purpose.

Sumpy Readmond suddenly assumed a mantle of responsibility and leadership. His mechanical ability stood out—for the first time he excelled at something. In his case it was the beginning of a career now under way. Teddy Adams, for another, taught himself to play the organ. Buddy Lewis, the broadcaster's spirited son, was already a skilled organist.

When expenses soared Choirmaster Lewis became Lecturer Lewis to raise funds. Then, the seemingly insurmountable problem of the "stop list" reared up. The "stop list" is the selection of pipes for various ranks, of which every pipe organ has many, including the flute, trumpet, oboe, chimes, vox humana, reed and diapason. Every rank contains a whole range of pipes, each with a different tone in much the same manner as a piano has a whole range of keys. Keen sensitivity is needed in the selection or the organs tones will be flat.

One day a visitor stood outside the Lewis door.

"Joe Whitefield!" Fulton Lewis cried as he spied his lawyer friend from Washington, D.C., "you're an answer to prayer."

Joe was an ardent and experienced amateur organist. He hardly had his coat off before he was down in the basement, listening to problems involving the "stop list." Snatched up by the fervor of this project, he forgot his mission, his job, everything, for days of continuous work. Together the kids and two grownups "voiced" over one thousand pipes, separating them into various ranks, testing them again and again for just the right sound.

Days later Joe Whitefield left, his eyes newly lighted from a labor of love. He went back to Washington, quit his career as lawyer and several weeks later phoned Lewis long distance.

"I never did like being a lawyer," he said. "I just needed to rub against some of the fervor of your kids to set me off on the right track. A man's a fool not to work at what he loves." Joe took a job with the Aeolian-Skinner Organ Co. of Boston.

Deadline for completion of the pipe organ was set for Christmas—in time for a Christmas Eve broadcast. Schedules were stepped up, and heads threatened to split over the confused jumble of wires, pipes, magnets, bellows, and connections. In November the process of moving all these from the Lewis basement to the church began.

Then it was discovered that part of the church would have to be redesigned before the organ would fit. Walls were knocked down and choir pews respaced. The organ chest was found to be the wrong size and would have to be rebuilt!

Lewis came home that night convinced he'd have to cancel the special broadcast. It was a grim household with little conversation and edgy nerves. After dinner, as both he and son Buddy often did when upset, Lewis sat down at his small electronic organ. He started to play jerkily, belligerent and bitter. Then the music softened. At the end, the powerful yet simple strains of "The Lord's Prayer" cast a hush over the whole house. It would be hard to imagine a more eloquent prayer for God's help and guidance.

The planned Christmas Eve broadcast was not cancelled. Instead, activity redoubled.

December 23rd was Black Thursday. The organ, though installed, needed endless adjustments. Choir members, drained of energy, beset with doubts, were completely listless. After dismissing them all with an optimism he didn't feel, Lewis worked far into the night and all the next day with the organ tuner.

Hours before the service was to start that December 24th, 1948, the little church by the side of the road began to fill. There was leathery Johnny Green, oysterman and blacksmith; old Doc Greenwell, still country doctor at 88; and some 200 others—all that could jam inside the small church. They came to hear a $35,000 pipe organ built by faith and tenacity. Would it play?

Lewis took his place at the organ and nodded to Mervill Dean, local merchant, who was stationed inside the organ loft to manipulate the swell shades that regulated the organ sounds. There hadn't been time to fix the automatic control.

At 7 p.m. the N.Y. radio technician nodded to Lewis. Then the soft strains of *Adeste Fidelis* floated through the church. Garbed in maroon and white gowns and black windsor ties, the junior choir marched down the aisle, their exultant voices joining the triumphant organ strains. Lewis, feeling the surging tones of the organ respond to his slightest touch, was lifted by the pride and devotion in the faces of his 30 "choir brats."

They had called these voices immature. If so, then the pipe organ was immature. Yet how could any voice or piece of craftsmanship be immature when created through long hours of work, discouragement, tears and grinding determination? Tonight their singing was reaching out across the country victoriously because this was music with love and heart and soul.

Organ builder skeptics were convinced, and the radio audience will never forget that broadcast. And parents looked upon their youngsters with new respect. That Christmas Eve a little bit of heaven itself crept into the church by the side of a road.

Illustration, Fulton Lewis, Jr., see page 173

TEEN-AGE PEN PALS

by BETTY BETZ

A suggestion for youth who want to do something specific to help bring world peace. Betty Betz is an authority and writer on teen-age problems.

AFTER RETURNING from a six months' flying trip around the globe to meet and write about the young people in foreign lands, I asked myself: "How can American teen agers help establish a foundation of peace?"

It seems that every country on the earth today regards the United States as the one and only powerful nation able to bring lasting peace to the rest of the world. There is one big goodwill job being done by young America without recognition, and that is "pen pals overseas."

Before I left on my trip, I frequently had requests from my readers for the names of young people in foreign countries. I felt it a great hobby for kids, but until I completed my world-wide assignment, I didn't realize that if *all* young Americans adopted the pen pal hobby, an inter-world exchange of letters among young people might actually be one big step toward world peace.

Much of the pen pals overseas correspondence originates in schools with geography class projects organized by intelligent teachers to give the student a personal contact with the rest of the world. There should be more—and in Sunday Schools too.

Fourteen-year-old Margaret McConnel of Eureka, Calif., recently invited Brenda Hill, her pen pal from Kent, England, to visit her in the United States. The two girls, who "knew" each other for years of writing, toured the country with the rest of the McConnel family. Brenda went back to England full of chocolate ice-cream sodas and enthusiasm for California red-wood trees and New York skyscrapers. Later I got a note from Margaret who visited Brenda's home in England. Their friend-ship is one of the best channels of understanding that could be.

After getting acquainted with kids from Bagdad to Berlin, I've found that youngsters who do not correspond with Amer-icans have a strange idea of what our country is like. More often than not they are given distorted pictures of the U.S.A. by those who work to undermine our country.

There are some tots who still believe the fabulous stories told about rich Americans who light their cigars with ten dollar bills. (On the other hand there are some Americans who still believe that Indian maharajahs drive around in Rolls Royces with diamond-studded wheels.) In reality, an Indian prince drives a Ford—if he's lucky!

The kids behind the Iron Curtain are told that Americans are war-mongering capitalists and that there are breadlines a mile long in the United States. Youngsters in foreign lands who see Grade B American movies often have a Hollywood picture of the U.S.A., complete with mink-lined swimming pools, glass cocktail bars, and a hot dog stand on every corner. Some foreign youngsters actually believe that gangsters and cowboys make up our chief population.

I visited several high schools in Japan where I was surprised to find the students learning to write and speak English. To date I have received over 4,000 letters from these same students re-questing American pen pals.

How shocked I was to meet many young friends the world over who told me they did not believe in God! Many of them did not even know about God, for they had no families or spiritual guidance. In the Communist-dominated countries, the government is trying to do away with the Church. The danger is with the young who are being indoctrinated not to believe in

God and the Ten Commandments. If our young Americans through their letters could encourage these young foreign children to build faith, it can make the future more hopeful.

The Communists are working tooth and nail on the minds of youth the world over. We Americans have the attitude that our way of life is so good that we don't need any sales talks to promote democracy. But sincere friendship and understanding among the young people of the world through exchange of gifts and letters can be more effective than any high pressure propaganda from the Soviet machine.

So let's have more pen pals overseas! If every foreign child throughout the world had an American friend—what a weapon that would be against Communism, and for peace!

Betty Betz (290 Park Avenue, New York City) will furnish names of Japanese youth who would like to correspond with American friends. For illustration of Miss Betz, see page 173

NEEDED—
ONE HOSPITAL WING

by LOUIS BRESCIA

Louis Brescia and his teen-ager friends from West-wood, New Jersey have one of the most effective answers to juvenile delinquency.

THE HEADLINES READ: "Juvenile killer caught. . . . Sixteen-year-old Victor Quero robbed the Apex Store last night, shot and killed the manager. . . ."

That was the story splashed over the front page one May morning in 1946—a day that made history out our way.

I didn't read on. The story had that old familiar ring—"teen-ager" always screamed at you in these write-ups. Being a teen-ager myself, I winced that always the wrongs of youth made the news, never the accomplishments. I said so outside class at our Park Ridge High School.

"We belong to a delinquent generation," drawled Beano indifferently. Beano was a cynic, leader of a crowd of young cynics. Handicapped by a poor family background, he seized every opportunity to bully his way into authority. Yet Beano had an honest, almost brutal frankness that made you like him.

"It's a crumby world," Beano shrugged. "The big shots don't know what to do about it—what do they expect of us?"

"What could we do?" I repeated to myself.

That night six of us—Paula Wagner, Philip Diamond, Ralph Myers, Frank English, my brother Vincent, and I—held council on our front porch. Big crime by teen-agers made the news—we wanted to make big news on the *good* side.

Paula, who long had had an ambition to be a nurse, suddenly remembered the desperate need for a hospital in our area. "Let's raise enough money to build a hospital—that's big enough," she blurted.

That was it. Everyone started to talk at once. You know how it is when an idea strikes home and all pitch in to make it grow.

Our enthusiasm couldn't be chilled by the next morning, gray as it was, or the forbidding prospect of approaching the Pascack Valley Hospital Association, organized since the war for the purpose of building a hundred-bed hospital in our area.

To the hospital trustees we simply offered to help raise funds and to perform other duties they might suggest. What a great idea it would be, we decided among ourselves, for them to name the hospital after our Teen-Ager Organization—that is, of course, after we had raised most of the $750,000 needed.

When the trustees had approved our setup, two of their number were appointed as Trustee Supervisors. We were asked, however, to stick to projects and leave to them the direct fund-raising from individuals in our area.

Afire with enthusiasm, we pitched in. A letterhead was drafted. Our slogan: "Teen-agers—A Million Strong—To Help the Cause Along." We split the area into four districts, then invited teen-agers from each district to become members.

Four teen-age officers were elected for the organization as a whole, and four more for each district—all kids we could count on. Funny how some fellas whom you figure will be of little help can change like magic when given a responsibility or a cause.

Our first job came quickly—a mailing of 17,000 letters by the Hospital Association to residents in the area. Our forces marshaled, work schedules set up, we sorted, enclosed, folded, addressed, sealed, stamped, and mailed the lot. Nothing glamorous, just *work*.

Soon after this first job, Beano sneered his reaction to our group.

"Kid's stuff. . . . You're lett'n a bunch of hospital people make errand boys outa ya. What d'ya get out of it? What's in it fer ya?"

Right there I wanted more than anything else to win Beano to our cause. "We're our own bosses," I came back. "We let the grown-ups help!"

Then I recalled Beano's ability for writing. "Hey, Beano," I cried. "Wanta help us with publicity?"

Before he could object, I hurriedly sketched the rough idea, thrust the paper with a brief explanation in his hand and beat it.

My first try with Beano was a failure, but I kept at it. I knew he watched us, sneers and all. Big shots among street-corner groups like his noticed their ranks thinning as many of the kids would hotfoot it to our outfit to work.

Soon we had organized spaghetti dinners, card parties, dances, and cake sales in different towns throughout the area. What a thrill to bank the first money earned! Each district set up its own bank account. Not a penny of any money collected was ever spent for entertainment or refreshments.

We became publicity agents for the Hospital Association as well as money raisers. One job, for example, called for mimeographing 6,900 circulars which we distributed throughout the schools for pupils to take home to their parents.

Experience came with each job. We discovered that the word "hospital" was a dud for publicity purposes, but "teen-agers" aroused interest, mainly, I'm afraid, because they expected teen-age stories to be sensationally bad.

Soon we had more projects almost than we could handle. Why not install coin boxes in stores, telling of the need for a new hospital in Bergen County? We made five hundred of them and placed them about strategically. Every few weeks we'd collect the money and leave thank-you notes.

We had just started work on a variety show when one morning

Beano stopped me. He handed me a layout for some publicity. It was a good job. "Not bad, Beano," I said, deliberately making little of it.

Beano wanted to say something, but couldn't seem to find the words. I had a sudden inspiration. "How about helping us with the *Questions and Answers* booklet?" I asked. Then I explained that we were preparing 1500 of them to distribute at meetings where hospital trustees spoke; and 13,000 for general distribution throughout the area.

His eyes kindled with interest, and I realized with a quick thrill that my big wish had come true—Beano was with us now. And after him came others who had been skeptical: athletes, school leaders in every field. The story of Beano is typical (although I altered his name and facts slightly so as not to embarrass anyone).

At the end of the first year results were tallied: $2600 earned. Out of this sum the site for the hospital was purchased.

Then we did make the papers! Even the *New York Times*. This was what we had dreamed of that May evening a year ago. But now somehow we didn't care too much whether or not *we* got notice; we just wanted the project to get publicity. Kids of other towns wrote to ask how we did it—they wanted to do the same! We could tell them.

There is no end to money-raising projects a group such as ours can find. A booth at the North Jersey Kennel Club Dog Show— where we sold catalogues and shares on a portable radio—netted us $615. We conducted a census in the towns of Emerson, Hillsdale, and Westwood for which a publishing house paid us $700.

Publicity projects included a skit put on in the local theater and three free concerts.

Second year income: $2,427.85. Two-years' receipts: $5,027.85.

Lately we have stepped up the membership drive, the figures now being 700 regular members and 1500 junior members. A regular member (age up to nineteen) pays dues of $1. Junior members (under thirteen) pay dues of 30c. Honorary members (over nineteen years of age) may contribute $5 or more.

Recently, we collected 10c admission fee at a model home which is on exhibit in Hillsdale. A system of hourly vigils was set up so that our teen-agers were on duty seven days a week. Handy & Allen, builders of the home, gave us this privilege.

Our pledge this year is for an added four-bed ward in the proposed hospital. The cost: $7200. This is about triple the amount we've taken in any one year to date. But we'll do it.

People think the answer to restless kids is youth centers with cokes, dances, and games. Sure—they're fine and needed. But somehow these don't seem to go far enough. Young people like to work for a cause, they want to be active in community projects. They like to be important. Give teen-agers a cause and they'll work their heads off.

Our main job is to build a hospital—yes. After a hospital is built, there will be other needy projects for us to tackle. And it goes deeper than that. By working for this hospital, we are working for the community, for the churches, for the schools—all the while training to become better citizens.

The churches are lending us wonderful support. Protestant, Catholic, and Jewish youth work together putting on dinners and affairs in churches of faiths different from their own. They are learning the real meaning of brotherhood. Increased church membership has been the result. We didn't start out with the idea we could make any spiritual contribution, but I guess every worthwhile path you take just naturally aids God's work.

Illustration, Louis Brescia, see page 173

PINT-SIZED PUBLISHER

by SHIRLEY JENKINS

*Big time newspaper editors had better keep their
eyes on this go-getter.*

IT STARTED with a fourth-grade assignment back in September
1951. Nine-year-old Stuart Jackson pounded the pavements of
Independence, Kansas, and wrote up local news items. Stuart
liked the assignment so much, he decided to put out a paper of
his own.

Six merchants bought ads at five cents each for the first issue
of *Stuart's Weekly*. At 3 cents a copy, it sold out completely.
Stuart dickered with his Dad for a mimeograph machine.
Terms: $2.00 a week.

Local news items and political comments were written in a
breezy, confidential style. A speech on high taxes brought such
table pounding that Stuart reported, "all the white meat flew
up off the plates." Other items included, "Mama got a beauty
treatment, but Daddy didn't see any difference" . . . "John Moon
got his dining room painted" . . .

Circulation boomed and ads jumped from six to over 50.
Samples: "Flock to Locks for Frocks" . . . "Dr. Wood won't hurt
you much" and "Happy feet with Neilson's Shoes."

Young Stuart collects news and ads all week long after school
hours, mimeographs his paper over weekends. It takes four
hours to cut the stencil alone. On Sundays, he and his six-year-
old brother, Michael, distribute the paper. Billy Schwenker
and Vernon Gaylor have been taken on as salesmen.

At the end of the first year, *Stuart's Weekly* had grown to
700 circulation, including 100 out-of-towners on the mailing list.
The Kansas City Star, The Pittsburg (Kansas) *Headlight Sun,*

Newsweek and other publications have quoted from Editor Jackson. Dogged enterprise, plus a sharp eye for cutting costs, have made the weekly a money maker. From the paper's income, Stuart has saved $350.

Does he dream of becoming a newspaper tycoon? Not at all. Stuart is saving his money for theological training. "My newspaper experience will help me in the ministry," he says, "and I may be able to write a religious column." Each Sunday part of his earnings goes to mission work.

Stuart, who is also a Lion Cub scout and likes sports, has the right approach. "Every Saturday we go to press—God and I," he writes.

Illustration, Stuart Jackson and brother Michael, see page 172

NO MORE
EMPTY WHEELBARROWS

by **KARL DETZER**

Headlines such as this used to cause great concern: "Boy dies of blood poisoning after fraternity initiation" . . . "Youth burned to death during hazing" . . . "Freshman loses eye . . ." Something new has been started recently to replace the old type of college "Hell Week."

A LANKY Hoosier athlete named Bob Lollar was striding across the campus of Indiana University one February morning in 1949 when he came upon a sight which annoyed him, and set him to thinking hard. Half a dozen young pledges to Greek letter fraternities were undergoing "Hell Week." Wearing freak haircuts and silly clothes, they were wasting vast quantities of energy pushing empty wheelbarrows, moving stone piles that had only to be moved back, making ridiculous spectacles of themselves. They were doing these absurd things merely to prove themselves worthy of wearing certain fraternity pins.

What was more, Lollar was about to become involved in similar harebrained goings-on. As "pledge trainer" for his own fraternity, Alpha Tau Omega, he was expected in the next few days to dream up silly antics for 20 youngsters. The more he thought about it the more unreasonable it seemed. The next day he walked into the office of a smart young assistant dean named Gary Schwartz.

"Look here, Gary," Lollar began earnestly. "The fraternities are wasting a lot of manpower and a lot of brains. Isn't there something constructive for these kids to do, some job on the campus that needs to be done? Why can't we make Hell Week into Help Week?"

Schwartz grabbed the idea. However, the campus was getting along nicely without the help of fraternity pledges. But he thought that the city of Bloomington, at the University gate, might not spurn offered aid. He called a minister friend. Indeed, there was a job to be done! The Christian Center, a community service building operated by half a dozen churches, was a drab old dwelling, much in need of paint.

Lollar called together his 20 pledges, explained his plan. The boys were enthusiastic. They bought, begged and borrowed paint brushes, wangled many gallons of paint from local merchants. Then at eight o'clock on a cold morning Alpha Tau Omega began its initiation with Lollar acting as foreman. The youngsters scrambled up ladders, scraped off the old paint, sanded the siding, slapped on a first coat. The next Saturday they finished the job.

"What next?" Lollar asked Dean Schwartz, who meanwhile had compiled a list of projects. Other fraternity chapters soon joined the movement—and Schwartz was ready to advise them. Within a few weeks the whole campus was alive with helpful efforts. Members of the Interfraternity Council fine-tooth-combed the city of Bloomington and the surrounding countryside. They found scores of jobs that needed to be done.

Spurred on by Dean Schwartz and more than a dozen Indiana fraternities, public officials, health and welfare groups, the chamber of commerce and churches submitted lists of needs. The Salvation Army reported a family, bogged down by illness, that lived in a house with a leaky roof. Lollar and his pledges soon were coaxing roofing and nails out of building dealers. At the end of a hard Saturday's work, the family had a new roof. But this time not only the pledges were on the job; older members of the fraternity joined them, knew the satisfaction of giving an appreciated helping hand.

On a cold winter morning Lollar and his crew tramped out into the country, hunting a house reported by the county welfare department. In it lived a widow with five small children. A relief truck had dumped a big load of stovewood beside the highway, an uphill mile from the widow's door. The young huskies of Alpha Tau Omega settled that problem fast. By noon, an armload at a time, they had carried the wood and stacked it neatly outside the woman's door.

Townspeople in Bloomington began to take notice. Maybe there was some sense in these wild fraternity kids, after all.

Within a year after Bob Lollar's crew painted the Christian Center, more than 20 of the 31 fraternities on the Hoosier campus were engaged in their own good works. Today, Help Week is universal at Indiana. Last year other midwest colleges went in for the new idea of initiations. Purdue, old-time football rival of Indiana, was first to follow its good example, then came Butler, Bowling Green and DePauw. Now the practice has spread to Cornell University and to schools in the south and far west. Everywhere Help Week was tried, the steadily growing opposition to college fraternities subsided. But at Indiana there has been a further spread of the good neighbor idea. Now, not only the pledges, but whole fraternity chapters go out together on helpful community jobs.

Sigma Chi discovered that the children of married students who occupy a big trailer court had no suitable place to play. Pledges, with plenty of help from their elder brethren, smoothed off a large vacant space in the center of the trailer village. They rolled and seeded it. Lumber and hardware dealers in the city once more gave a hand. The boys built swings and teeter-totters, painted them, and set them up. Today the new playground is used by children from the whole neighborhood.

Indiana's Sigma Alpha Mu runs a baby-sitting service with members as well as pledges on call. The head of the University's home economics department instructed all 60 of them in the mysteries of diaper folding and pinning; now their expert care is in great demand. They charge 50 cents an hour, give all proceeds to charity.

Fraternity boys painted the city bandshell, a long, hard job. They cut grass in the parks. Last fall leaves from Bloomington's thousands of shade trees filled the streets, making a fire hazard. City crews could not get rid of them fast enough. So a gang of husky young men from the fraternity houses helped out with brooms, rakes and shovels.

Indiana's fraternity men use their brains and peculiar skills. One group took as its project the rehabilitation of a Boy Scout camp near Bloomington. The pledge trainer happened to be the son of a quarryman in the state's rich limestone belt. He had worked summers for his father, knew how to handle stone-cutter's tools.

He talked quarry owners into donating several large blocks of stone and the fraternity paid the freight and hauling charges. At the camp, with borrowed tools, the trainer instructed his pledges in the details of cutting limestone slabs. With the slabs they paved a 20 by 30 foot terrace in front of the clubhouse, a job that would have cost the Scouts many hundreds of dollars.

Bloomington's Mayor Tom Lemon says, "These kids are on the right track today. Police don't have any more trouble with them. The townspeople have a new feeling toward the campus. We're working together and getting on fine."

Hell Weeks are on the wane all over America. The Indiana faculty, after watching the new spirit at work for more than two years, is convinced that the Greek letter societies have come of age. They say that the GI students, who brought sophistication and serious purpose to school, probably are greatly responsible for the new attitude.

Bob Lollar, who started it all at Indiana, was a veteran. To men who had been through real Hell, "Hell Week" seemed silly.

Illustration, fraternity work project, see page 173

THEY EARNED
THEIR OWN LIBRARY

by RUTH HYATT

> *What can happen when youngsters pool their imaginations.*

THE SCHOOL population of Fitchburg is around 7,000. Since library facilities were inadequate back in 1947, the youngsters were asked: "Do you want a special youth library?"

Surprisingly, they answered, "It won't be ours unless we do the work. Let us raise the money."

The children took hold of the project eagerly. There are 27 schools in the city. Each elected representatives and a promotion committee was formed. They set their own goal at $10,000.

Donald Guenette, who cooks supper at night for his working parents, managed a job from 3 to 5 every day to earn his share.

Together, Ronald Moilanen and Cecil Glode, 3rd graders, earned $91.75, selling seeds, soap and fishworms. Their dream: an auditorium, especially for story-telling.

Arthur S. Taylor, Jr., 10 years old, spoke before 350 Elks who then helped organize a paper drive.

Donald Heikkinen made sequin earrings. His profits would help provide special reading tables.

Bruce Bishop picked and sold pussy willows. He was inspired by the plans for the library garden.

The 34 captains marshalled students in their respective schools; their campaign built steadily until the goal was topped by $381.75.

Parents gladly joined their children's cause by pledging the remaining necessary funds. In the fall of 1950 the Youth Library opened its doors, built for, and by, the youth of a town whose adults had had the rare insight to throw them the ball—and then cheer them on.

Illustration, Fitchburg youngsters, see page 172

HIGH VOLTAGE
ON THE CAMPUS

by **HARTZELL SPENCE**

*What are the six questions asked most by college stu-
dents? Here's a picture of spiritual changes taking
place on American campuses, written by a top writer
who has done considerable research on the subject.*

IF YOU SHARE the widespread anxiety that America's college generation is preponderantly godless—forget it! The truth is that
our youth has generated a dynamic religious surge in recent
years. It is a factor in breaking down campus discrimination.
It has caused thousands of young people to volunteer for summer social service throughout the world. It has resulted in a
minor revolution in academic approaches to religious teaching.

This movement has not been brought down on the heads of
young people by persistent adults, but has burst forth out of
students' own interests.

The youthful search for God has influenced educators, even
in public schools. Dr. Gordon Sproul, president of the University
of California, stated recently, "It is questionable whether we are
right in avoiding the entire subject of religion and leaving this
wholly to the church and the family. Out of this neglect has
come a very serious thing, namely our neglect of youth's capacity for faith."

Student attitudes have compelled educators to face up to the
reality of God in the lives of men. Instead of ignoring religious
challenges in classroom discussions, teachers in large numbers
are now interpreting such questions wherever they arise, from
physics and astronomy to history and literature. New textbooks
in the arts and sciences since 1948 reflect this change.

According to a study made among teachers by the University
Christian Mission, five of the most persistent student questions

are these: How do we know there is a God?... If God is loving and kind, why is there so much suffering in the world?... Can one be a Christian without belonging to a church?... Is Jesus divine?... Is it wrong for a Christian student to have premarital sex relations?

How do educators answer such posers? A professor of philosophy at the University of Illinois, challenged with the existence of God, responded with a query of his own: "How do you know there isn't?"

The class came to life, and for forty-five minutes the students sought to clarify their own beliefs. The problem unresolved in class, the professor met his students that night at the student union and continued the debate until the building closed three hours later.

Professors who are not afraid to answer searching spiritual questions from students find themselves much sought after. Professor George F. Thomas, Princeton's professor of religious thought, was voted the most popular teacher on the campus in 1943. A similar accolade was bestowed on Dr. Hans Frei, professor of religion at Wabash College, Indiana. Denver University students spontaneously campaigned recently for the election of their chaplain, Dr. Glenn A. Olds, as university chancellor. He was the one man they felt best understood their problems.

Other teachers awakened to new religious experience by the searching queries of pupils have taken temporary leave to enroll in theological seminaries, where they can study religion in relation to their own teaching assignments. Some 135 professors from 39 states, few of whom taught theology, gathered in the summer of 1953 at Nashville, Tenn., to examine their own spiritual lives in the light of classroom inquisitiveness.

Students by the thousands, dissatisfied with selfish materialism, formed a "Creative Use of Summer" movement, gave of themselves at their own expense. For example, one summer 25 went to a Mexican village and by hand labor built a school and a sewerage system for the town.

The Methodist Church, alone, found such service for over 1,000 students. The American Friends Service Committee, the Student YMCA and YWCA, and a dozen other agencies enrolled thousands more. A group of 150 took summer government jobs in Washington and spent their evenings in discussion of questions involving government and diplomacy.

One significant upsurge has been in one of the least likely locales: the land-grant colleges, often called the "godless state universities." Supported by public funds, these universities have traditionally shunned religious emphasis as contrary to the First and Fourteenth Amendments to our Constitution, which define the separation of Church and State. The students, however, are rejecting the separation thesis. Many of them contend that the founding fathers meant freedom *for* religion, not freedom *from* it.

In 1952, regents of the University of Minnesota took a bold step. School funds (provided by state taxes) were used to promote religious activities within the University. Certain citizens demanded this be stopped and invoked court action, but the Minnesota Supreme Court upheld the University, refusing to compel the school regents to justify the use of tax money when so used for religious activities. The Minnesota case may yet go to the Supreme Court of the United States.

A clear interpretation of the controversy is inevitable. Today only two of the 65 largest land-grant colleges do not now make provision for campus religious activity. Before World War II, 56 of these institutions had no such provision. And a recent survey at 32 of these schools revealed that 90 per cent of the students regarded God as a vital influence in their lives.

Over 1,000 religious organizations today maintain permanent staffs on college campuses. There are 300 full-time college chaplains (compared to 20 back in 1941).

New chapels have been built at such secular schools as Kansas State, which has just completed a chapel with three altars, and the University of Maryland, which provides thirteen offices for chaplains of various faiths. On the campus of Louisiana State University, a large and beautiful Baptist Student Center has recently been built. Where large chapels are available, as at Syracuse University, Penn State, Yale, Duke, Cornell and Leland Stanford, student attendance on Sunday is regularly between 900 and 1,000.

Another trend to watch is the development of student churches on the campus. The Lutherans have already set up 32, run by students, for students, but responsible to the local district church. A young pastor (probably just out of school himself) is on hand to advise and counsel.

Said one member of the Calvary Lutheran Chapel at Wisconsin University, "I'm a lot more active here in the church than I ever would be at home."

A significant point: many students are coming to realize that religion is more than a study course (like history) or a form of group worship, but something to experience personally. Burrill Dinhens, a junior at Asbury College, Kentucky, reported an experience while alone at prayer in his college chapel.

"As a college student, I know what a need there is for a quiet place to pray," he said. "So many times the local churches are locked . . . or there are other things to keep people out. I now feel called by God to work for the establishment of prayer rooms or chapels, non-denominational and open 24 hours a day, upon the campuses of every American college and university."

The annual Religious Emphasis Week, now in 65% of all U.S. colleges on a purely voluntary basis, is a good test of student interest. The University Christian Mission, which conducted forty of these "Weeks" last year, thoroughly covers campus life. At the University of Oklahoma, for example, a team of twelve began in local churches on a Sunday, and within a week had entered 85 classrooms, addressed 11,160 persons at convocations, and had led "bull sessions" in 56 fraternities, sororities and dormitories.

"I found," said one of the team, "an almost plaintive interest in God."

The religious beliefs of college students, according to a post-World War II survey made by Gordon Allport and others at Harvard and Radcliffe (confirmed independently at Princeton), were disturbing to conventionalists. Of those queried 70 percent admitted the need for a personal religious life. And 70 percent also found no appreciable conflict between science and religion.

But this may shock you: only 25 percent of non-Catholic students questioned admitted to orthodox religious beliefs; 57 percent rejected denominationalism; 50 percent rejected the divinity of Christ, but not that of God; and only 25 percent believed in personal immortality.

The analysts pointed out, however, that "Although there was a loss of orthodoxy and formal religious participation, an interest grew in the social aims of religion, in the problem of evil, of immortality, and of the existence of God."

But, characteristically of youth, the college generation now appears to be taking in its own hands the search for enlightenment and faith. Youth wants inspiration, a faith to live by. And the 300 college chaplains will tell you, unequivocally, that youth is beginning to find what it seeks.

Illustration, students decorate chapel, see page 173

WHAT

CAN

HAPPEN

THROUGH

PRAYER

PAGE 227

PAGE 233

PAGE 202

PAGE 230

PAGE 224

PAGE
220

PAGE 208

PAGE 204

PAGE 217

IT HAPPENED
IN A COFFEE SHOP

by CELESTIN SIBLEY

They were all strangers until the little girl spoke up

THE LUNCH counter had that stainless steel and nickel shine indigenous to lunch counters—and in the soft early morning light it looked clean and impersonal but sort of cheerful.

Twenty odd citizens were lined up on the stools. There were college students, a somber-looking man with a brief case, two young nurses, a little rumpled and hollow-eyed after a night on duty at the nearby hospital, a family with a little girl and a sullen teen-ager impartially distributing lipstick between her coffee cup and cigarette.

The lunchroom was quiet except for the occasional sharp crack of an egg shell in the counterman's expert hand, the sputter of frying bacon and the bored voice of a customer, ordering more coffee.

The customers were engrossed in their own thoughts—inconspicuous, anonymous, brought together by nothing more binding than the tribal custom of eating in the morning. They did not even have real hunger in common . . . just eating because people do.

And then at the end of the counter the little girl said in a carrying voice, "Mother, don't we ask the blessing here?"

The counterman stopped wiping the already spotless counter and grinned at her suddenly.

"Sure we do, sister," he said. "You say it."

She bowed her smooth little head. The young counterman turned and glanced firmly at his customers and bowed his head, too. Up and down the counter heads went down, the nurses, the

students, the man with the brief case and then, slowly, the teen-
ager.

The breathless little voice was loud in the room:

"God is great, God is good. Let us thank Him for our food.
By His hand we are fed, He gives to us our daily bread. Amen."

Heads went up along the counter. Eating was resumed but
somehow the atmosphere had subtly changed. The man with the
brief case smiled and remarked to the nurses that he had a new
baby in their hospital. Conversation became general.

The counterman smiled at the students and said, "Well, I
won't be seeing you after this week. I reckon I'm going to
Korea." They paused, paying their check, to talk with him
about it. Somehow a tenuous bond of friendliness and mutual
confidence had grown up in the room and the little girl, ob-
livious to what she had done, lathered her waffle with syrup
and ate it happily.

Illustration, Celestin Sibley, see page 201

ON HIS OWN TWO FEET

by **GRACE PERKINS OURSLER**

The eyes of parents and son met and held. In a moment of crisis they made a decision beyond common sense.

THE BOY HAD FALLEN, running home after school, and skinned his left knee. It was no more than a scratch—there wasn't even a rent in his trousers—but by night the knee started to ache. Nothing much, he thought, being 13 and the sturdy son of a frontiersman. Ignoring the pain, he knelt in his nightgown and said his prayers, then climbed into bed in the room where he and his five brothers slept.

His leg was painful the next morning, but he still did not tell anyone. The farm kept the whole family relentlessly busy; always he had to be up at six to do his chores before school. And he must be thorough about them or he would be sent back to do them over again, no matter what else he had to miss, including meals. In their household, discipline was fair but stern.

Two mornings later the leg ached too badly for him to drag himself to the barn. That was a Sunday and he could remain behind, while the rest of the family drove into town. School homework finished, he sat in the parlor rocker, examining and comparing the three family Bibles; one in German that held the records of all their births and deaths; another in Greek that was his father's proud possession and finally the King James version shared by mother and all the sons.

One night this week it would be the boy's turn to lead the family devotions. He could select his own passages from the Old

With credit to Soldier of Democracy *by Kenneth S. Davis (Doubleday).*
Copyright also by Reader's Digest Association.

and New Testaments and read them aloud and try to get a discussion going; sometimes they became exciting. But now the pain blurred his attention; he put aside the Scriptures and dozed until his brothers returned from Sunday school.

Mom and Dad did not come home with them because Sunday was parents' day off; the boys did the housework and cooked the big meal of the week, while father and mother stayed on for church service.

But by the time dinner was ready the boy had climbed into bed. The shoe had to be cut off his swollen and discolored leg. Why on earth hadn't he told somebody? Go quick and fetch the doctor!

Mother bathed knee and foot and thigh, applied poultices and wiped the boy's sweating forehead with a moist, cool cloth. She was an intense and vital woman. Confronted with this angry infection, her manner remained serene. Mom had nursed her brood through accidents and ailments from toothaches to scarlet fever; one son she had lost, but that only made her calmer and more determined when she had to fight for the others.

Old Dr. Conklin examined the leg and pursed his lips. "It's not likely we can save it!"

The invalid sat up stiffly. "What's that mean?" he asked huskily.

"It means," explained the doctor gently, "if things get worse we'll have to amputate."

"Not me!" stormed the boy. "I won't have it! I'd rather die!"

"The longer we wait, the more we will have to take off," urged the doctor.

"You won't take any off!" The boy's voice broke with an adolescent crack, as his mother turned away, shaken. But there was no adolescence in the eyes that defied the doctor's reproachful gaze.

Dr. Conklin stalked out, nodding to the mother to follow him.

As he stood in the hallway explaining to both parents about what could and probably would happen, they could hear the boy calling for his brother: "Ed! *Ed!* Come up here, will you?"

The brother stamped in and then they heard the sick lad's voice, high pitched with pain: "If I go out of my head, Ed, don't let them cut off my leg. Promise me, Ed—*promise!*"

In a moment Ed came out and ran to the kitchen. When he returned his mother said, "Ed, what's your brother asking for?"

"Fork! To bite on; keep from screaming."

Then Edgar stood outside the bedroom door, his arms folded. Quite clearly he was standing on guard.

Ed looked straight at old Dr. Conklin. "Nobody's going to saw off that leg!" he announced.

"But, Ed—you'll be sorry," gasped the doctor.

"Maybe so, Doc. But I gave him my word."

And nothing changed that.

If Ed had not stood his ground, father and mother might have yielded. They were not yet convinced that amputation was necessary; they were doubtful. The adamant attitude first of the sick boy and then of his brother was incredible, for defiance of parental authority was unknown in this household. Yet there was Ed, standing before the sickroom door.

"Guess we'll wait and see how he looks by tonight, eh, Doc?" said the father.

For two days and nights Ed stood guard, sleeping at the threshold, not leaving even to eat. The fever mounted, and the suffering boy babbled in torment, but the older brother showed no weakening of resolve, even though the discoloration of the swollen leg was creeping toward the pelvis, just as the doctor had predicted. Ed remained firm because he had given his promise, and also because he shared the frontiersmen's horror of being less than physically perfect.

The parents knew that their son would never forgive an

amputation, and Ed's attitude continued to be decisive, time after time, when the doctor returned. Once, in helpless rage, Dr. Conklin shouted, "It's murder!" and slammed the front door. Nothing but a miracle could save the boy now!

Mother, father and watchful brother Ed shared the same thought, as their anxious eyes turned from the doorway. Had they forgotten their faith in the turmoil of their fears? Why, this sick boy's grandfather, that vigorous and inspiring old farmer-minister who had been leader of the River Brethren Colony in Pennsylvania, had always believed in healings wrought by faith. Now, in this desperate hour, the three went to their knees at the bedside.

They prayed, taking turns in leading one another. Father, mother—and at last Edgar—would rise and go about the farm work and rejoin the continual prayer. During the second night the other four brothers would kneel from time to time and join in the prayers.

The next morning, when the faithful old doctor stopped by again, his experienced eye saw a sign. The swelling was going down! Dr. Conklin closed his eyes and made a rusty prayer of his own—a prayer of thanksgiving. Even after the boy dropped into a normal sleep, one member of the family after another kept the prayer vigil.

It was nightfall again and the lamps were lighted when the boy opened his eyes. The swelling was away down now, and the discoloration had almost faded. In three weeks—pale and weak, but with eyes clear and voice strong—the boy could stand up.

And Ike Eisenhower was ready to face life.

Illustration, President Dwight D. Eisenhower, see page 201

THAT EXTRA BOOST

by BOB RICHARDS

The story of a delinquent boy who became the Olympic and World champion pole vaulter. What chance remark by a girl helped change his life? What source of energy enabled this athlete-minister (also an Associate Professor at LaVerne College) to rise from a sickbed to make his winning jump?

PEOPLE OFTEN ASK me if prayer "works." I'm not sure whether they are asking me as a pole vaulter or a minister. It doesn't really matter as the answer is the same. Through prayer I have done things that otherwise would have been impossible.

Two of the best jumps of my life have come as a direct result of prayer. Once in Finland several years ago, I was sent to the hospital with a strep throat two days before the big meet. All Thursday and Friday I lived on a diet of penicillin and nothing else. Saturday morning my arms were so tired I could hardly do a push up. Nevertheless, I had been asked to try and compete.

Up to the time they put the cross bar into position, I was praying for strength. I cleared the bar at just under 15 feet, the highest jump of my life to that very minute.

Again in 1951 I found myself worn out, depleted mentally and physically just before the Chicago Relays. Was it wise for me to fly East to a meet in which I didn't think I could offer my best? With the question came my immediate answer . . . the expense money and tickets. So I went.

The plane left Los Angeles at 8:30 in the morning and arrived in Chicago at 7:00 that night . . . just time for me to make the event. Instead of sleeping on the flight, I spent the time in prayer.

That night I barely missed the World's Record. My jump went down as 15 feet, 4⅞ inches.

To me, those are answered prayers. And I don't mean God giving me the edge over the other fellow—for I never pray for victory and I always pray for my opponents as well as myself.

What I do mean is that prayer is our point of contact with a very real power within, that releases the energy necessary for us to turn in the highest performance of which we are capable.

Is pole vaulting important enough to command that power? Everything and anything is.

It's like leaven. Once you contact it, it infuses every activity. In my case the sports field *has* been important. It has given me a passport with youth throughout the country . . . and it has introduced me to the qualities we must all humbly seek if we would live like champions.

Youngsters are demanding, practical. "If I learn to pray," they say, "If I learn to contact this power, if I accept the discipline that is required . . . where am I?"

Then I can show them that the qualities that have made great champions have made them tremendous not only in athletics, but in life itself.

Dean Cromwell, for 40 years track coach at the University of Southern California, when he addressed his Olympic team headed for London in 1948, told us straight, "If you can't win fairly, don't win."

He reminded us that a clean, fit body and a clean, fit mind were essential. It would require work and discipline to render each man a fit vessel to fulfill our prayers. In that degree, God would help those who helped themselves.

"Like the two little girls who were afraid they'd be late for school one morning," Cromwell said. "One had an idea. 'Let's stop and pray.' But the other had a better idea: 'Oh, no. Let's keep running and pray as we run.'"

His team ran and prayed and they weren't late ... they came back covered with Olympian glory.

The champion who relies on a Power greater than himself dares to believe he can do ever better. Because he is aware that the Power is not his own, he puts no limits on it. Thus records go on being smashed, men run faster, jump higher, until they are *proving* that this power is limitless, bounded only by what each individual believes he can do.

Dutch Warmerdam, a man who recognized the power of prayer, was told that a pole vaulter would never clear 15 feet. In four years, between 1940 and '44, Warmerdam did it 43 times.

Faith and confidence, as well as hard work, turned tragedy into victory for Glenn Cunningham. As a kid Glenn was badly burned saving his brother from a schoolhouse fire. His legs received the worse burns and healed slowly, covered with stiff ugly scar tissue. For a while no one believed he would walk again. With infinite patience and faith he began teaching himself ... working behind a plow ... until he could take a few steps. Then walk. Then trot. The training was long and arduous. The scar tissue never disappeared from his legs. But Glenn Cunningham became one of the greatest milers who ever lived.

Here you can offer proof positive to young people that the qualities of discipline, faith, prayer, carry them up the path they want to travel. I know that well for I needed to find it out myself.

As a kid in Champaign, Illinois, I ran around with a gang that I suppose was tougher than most. We fought daily, swore a lot, stole fruit now and then. I don't think we ever stopped to wonder where all this might lead.

Then, because some girl in high school made a crack about wanting a "Christian boy friend" it suddenly occurred to me that I hadn't been to church in 10 years. That high school girl, believe me, was a true worker for Christ. I didn't dash off at once

. . . not by a long shot. But one Sunday morning weeks later, when I was reading comics and listening to the radio, I had a sudden overwhelming desire to go to church. I didn't stop to ask myself why. I didn't even stop to put on my tie. I just went straight to the Church of the Brethren that I remembered passing in the neighborhood.

Here the minister, the Reverend Merlin Garber, began telling me about this other path, the one of discipline, faith, prayer. He told me where it led. It sounded good. Five of the fellows in our crowd later went to jail for holding up a gas station. It wasn't hard to figure which was the better way.

That, I suppose, was my conversion. But understanding didn't follow immediately.

There's no telling how long I might have floundered about if a friend of mine, a young preacher, hadn't told me a story about his first sermon.

Charlie was a young man who was pretty sure of himself, proud of his self-sufficiency. When an older preacher warned him that his first sermon might be tough, Charlie just laughed.

"But, Charlie," said the older man, "it might. Words just might not come. If that happens try taking a Bible phrase and hold fast to it. Repeat it until God stabilizes your mind and you get the blessing and inspiration *from* Him."

Independent Charlie just laughed again. "I won't have any trouble." But he did.

Faced with his first big audience his mind went blank. From nowhere came the old minister's words. He had said, "until *God* stabilizes your mind and you get the inspiration and blessing *from Him.*" From those words Charlie drew his strength. He got his help. And that thought began to help me.

Maybe my mistake, too, was being too sure of *myself,* too proud of my self-sufficiency.

That was the beginning of my understanding, an understanding which gave me the earnest desire to become a minister myself; without that I'd probably have gone right on following my own will.

Each one of us has to catch up someday with the wisdom of Paul the Apostle, who admitted frankly that the good he wanted to do he could not, while the evil he didn't wish to do, that he did . . . *until* he found he could "do all things through Christ which strengtheneth me." *

The answer doesn't lie in any change outside the individual. The first change has to come within the heart of man . . . his concept of himself, his concept of God and prayer. Where man has failed God *has* provided an answer. Where we are weak He is strong.

The history of the greatest champion who ever lived, Jesus, has proven that, once and for all. And Jesus invited us to follow "the Way, the Truth, and the Life."

Many of Jesus' victories were major ones. Certainly He dared to do the "impossible."

His advice would apply to any athlete today. Christ insisted:
On clean living . . . "the pure in heart."
On hard work . . . "no man that puts his hand to the plow and looks back is worthy . . ."
On faith . . . "whatsoever ye ask, believing . . ."
On confidence . . . "Fear not, little flock, it is your Father's good pleasure to *give* you the Kingdom."

Certainly He came through when the pressure was on. Instantly and before multitudes He healed the sick, fed five thousand, raised the dead. Then He instructed those who followed Him to contact that same power.

"Follow thou Me . . ." "Greater works than these shall *ye* do." He told us that the Kingdom of Heaven was *within* us, that the power of a champion was there, available to us all.

Illustration, Bob Richards and wife Mary, see page 201

WHAT EVERY FATHER SHOULD KNOW

by DR. DANIEL A. POLING

The experience of the famous four chaplains of World War II is an epic in American history. Here's the intimate personal story of one of these chaplains, as told by his father.

THE TELEGRAM had a solemn, urgent tone. I was to meet the train at Grand Central Station and "say nothing to Mother." It was from Clark Poling, my youngest son, who was fifteen years old at the time and away at Oakwood School.

I wondered what kind of a jam my boy might be in. By the time I had met Clark and we had closeted ourselves in my office, I was going through one of the most uncertain moments of my life.

"Dad," he began, "what do you know about God?"

That was all. I was relieved, but checked an impulse to show it. Who can tell what tumultuous emotions, inner uncertainties and fears lie behind such a question?

What *did* I know about God? I'm glad I didn't have time to prepare my answer. For what I said came from the heart and not the head.

"Clark," I said, "I know mighty little about God. But what I do know by test and experience—sickness and health, sorrow and joy, death and life—controls my whole life."

I told him how temptations and wrong impulses came to me as they do to everyone . . . in every relationship and decision— that we may make mistakes, yet through faith in God we can be guided to do the right thing.

For three hours we talked, then we went home where a surprised mother welcomed us and soon had us seated before a steaming home cooked meal.

Clark Poling later worked out his own answer to the question: How can I know God? He wrote:

". . . through Jesus Christ! and, of course, through prayer, Bible study and service to men, women and children. God is a Being so great and good that when we are rightly related to Him, we are spiritually prepared for whatever experiences we have to meet."

He was to demonstrate its truth too!

June with its emphasis on Father's Day, reminds me how both as a father, and now as a grandfather, I usually learn more from my children than they do from me. And parents have so much to live up to! What the father does, more than what he says, will determine his son's actions in life.

Clark was four when I took him to have his tonsils removed. His struggles and cries had become so violent in the doctor's office that I had to lift him in my arms and pin his limbs to his sides.

Suddenly he was completely calm.

"Daddy, will you stay all through?" he asked with a searching look. I said I would.

Later the doctor nodded to tell me that he was under the anesthetic, and I could leave. At the door, I remembered my promise. "*He* wouldn't know, Doctor, but I would." So I stayed to the finish.

When the boy's eyes fluttered open, I grinned reassuringly. "Daddy, you did stay through, didn't you?" he said weakly. I was very glad I had the right answer. A small point, some may say, yet now I feel somehow that youngsters see through most small deceits by parents, and little dishonesties can build barriers between parent and child.

Clark played football in college, was outstanding in debates, yet I felt sure he was always irresistibly heading for the ministry. Both my sons were born to a preaching tradition. For six generations, with but one exception, my forebears have been clergymen. Their parishes have ranged from New England to the Pacific Coast. Always, however, the decision to preach came from some inner conviction.

I'll never forget a certain night Clark and I spent in a Detroit hotel in 1931. I was there to make an address and Clark had come down from school to be with me.

It was late when we retired in our twin beds. I was tired, but he wanted to talk. Several times I was on the verge of asking him to turn it off (as you often had to do with him). Then suddenly it occurred to me that he wanted to tell me something, and that it was through such informal, natural moments that father and son best express their love, share confidences and create the type of relationship that transcends all others.

Quietly, but so impressively that as long as I live I shall remember the electric-like shock with which I heard him speak the words, he flung his arm across my bed and I felt his hand over my chest: "Daddy, I'm going to preach. I've *got* to do it!"

I wasn't sleepy or tired then. I knew that this was what I had always wanted. We talked until dawn.

There was much of the unconventional in Clark's ministry. One moment he would be swinging a pick on a road, or helping some of the boys clear away boulders. Minutes later, after slipping on shirt and coat, he would be leading a religious conference with assurance and vigor.

He and his charming wife, Betty, made a perfect team during the five years they spent in Schenectady, tirelessly helping to rebuild their church into one of the most active religious centers in the community.

Shortly after Pearl Harbor, Clark enlisted in the Chaplain's Corps.

After months of training and duty, the day came when Clark was to leave on the troop transport "Dorchester." We had dinner together in Boston—Clark, his wife, Betty, their son, Corky, and myself. I saw him last at the bus station. All fathers of Servicemen know that final glimpse of their boys' faces at such partings . . . Then the bus was gone and it was dark, but Clark's farewell smile stays with me.

Their common love of God brought the four chaplains together during that now well-known night of dark terror on board the torpedoed "Dorchester" back in 1943. The world thrilled to the story. After giving away their own life jackets, the chaplains stood with their arms locked, praying for the safety of the wrecked men to the end. One survivor told of hearing Clark Poling's contagious and calming laugh only minutes before the ship went down.

Illustration, Daniel A. Poling, see page 200

I LEARNED HOW
PRAYER IS ANSWERED

by ALICE MARBLE

When Alice Marble, famous tennis champion, awoke on what had promised to be the most exciting Saturday of her life, she couldn't move. Yet there is a superhuman power within everyone which can be tapped in an emergency, as this outstanding athlete discovered.

Wimbledon, to a tennis player, compares with the Metropolitan for the opera singer. One who wins at Wimbledon is considered champion of the world. I had previously made two unsuccessful trips and knew that if I were going to win I would have to do it this particular year.

I managed to get to the finals in all three events. Here promised to be the most exciting Saturday of my life. I wasn't a bit concerned about having to play the three finals in one day.

The big Saturday dawned or rather, it crashed with a bang, for I couldn't get out of bed. I screamed at my teacher, Eleanor "Teach" Tennant: "I'm hurt."

She thought my paralysis stemmed from sheer excitement. But as she tried to help me out of bed she, too, realized that I couldn't navigate. Always efficient in an emergency Teach called our friend, Dr. Dunning, who came running.

I had torn a stomach muscle and he advised me not to play, saying that I would undoubtedly do some permanent harm. When I insisted that I would play he said he would take no responsibility for my foolishness.

Dr. Dunning then bound my middle with heavy adhesive and was about to leave when I said rather brusquely, "Please take it off."

The doctor thought I had taken leave of my senses, but acquiesced. I explained my reasons to him—that perhaps the excitement of playing on the center court would make me forget the injury; that I didn't want to be reminded by the pull of the adhesive.

After the doctor left I couldn't look at the disappointment on Teach's face. I asked her to help me dress as I wanted to go down to the lobby of the hotel. She finally agreed, probably because she, too, wanted to be alone. It meant as much to her, my trainer, as to me. My success meant much to many who had invested years of faith in me.

All the way down in the elevator I thought, "I must at least make an appearance on the court." I was to be in three of the four finals. Twenty thousand English fans would be there: five thousand had camped on the grounds overnight for the privilege of standing all afternoon to watch the tennis.

In the lobby of the hotel, our genial manager, Mr. Burdet, rushed over, all smiles until he saw my face. I told him what had happened and asked if I might use his suite for an hour or more as I wanted to be alone. He personally escorted me upstairs and silently left the room.

I found myself thinking of my mother who had died the year before. I remembered the hundreds of times we had heard her say, "Trust in the Lord." In my despair I had forgotten all about Him. Then I did a strange thing; strange because I had never done it before. Mother had always allowed us to say our prayers any way we liked. We didn't kneel formally.

But now, injury and all, I got down on my knees and prayed to God not to let me make a fool of myself on the court that afternoon. I never asked Him to let me win. I asked Him that I would not let my supporters down.

Somehow I felt better and stronger, and able to face Teach and to tell her that everything would be all right. I rose feeling calm and sure in spite of pain.

Neither of us could eat the lunch sent to our rooms nor did we speak a single word in the car as we drove out to Wimbledon.

Ordinarily I warmed up for half an hour before an important match but of course the warm-up was forsaken that day. As I sat in the little cubicle Teach laced my shoes as it was impossible for me to reach up or down. At the given moment the official escort, Teddy Tinling, escorted my opponent, that grand gal, Kay Stammers, and me to the center court.

I let Kay toss her racket to decide the service. She won and elected to receive. The idea of having to reach up to serve was frightening.

How can I explain two selves? My bodily self was agonized and in terror. My inner self was secure and above body: All that I knew or felt was Trust in the Lord.

After the short warm-up period of two minutes allotted by the umpire, we began. I shall never forget as long as I live that first game. Each swing of the service made me want to scream. The score went to deuce four times before I won the game. Then, from the moment we changed courts on that odd game, I did not, for an instant, remember the torn muscle. Twenty-five minutes later I had won the championship of the world.

Then came the biggest thrill of all. Kay and I were presented to Queen Mary, considered Wimbledon's patron saint. I was proud and happy and grateful.

Yet I wanted to be alone. Success was very sweet and very sobering when the first breathtaking excitement was over. During the next few days that I spent in bed I had plenty of time to reflect upon my victory and to realize that despite my years of work and preparation, I was merely the medium of a Greater Power. He looks after us if we only give Him half a chance.

Illustration, Alice Marble, see page 201

WHAT IS
UNCLE SAM'S PRAYER?

by **CONRAD HILTON**

> *A boy wrote a letter to the head of a vast hotel organ-*
> *ization—about prayer. It produced an amazing*
> *chain reaction.*

EARLY Thursday morning on February 5, 1953 a car pulled away from the White House and the President of the United States directed the driver—*to go to a prayer meeting.*

I was on hand to see President Eisenhower, Justices of the Supreme Court, Senators, Congressmen, bow their heads together in prayer at that breakfast. I saw protocol swept aside and Vice President Nixon, Supreme Court Justices and diplomats drop into any empty seat among the 500 guests.

To be host to such a gathering was a great honor for me. To see the enlarged picture of Uncle Sam (shown on front cover) dominate the Mayflower Hotel ballroom, to hear that room hushed in prayer—it all seemed like a miracle.

Sitting there, I thought back to the day, two years before, when a letter came to my office, a small envelope nearly lost in a stack of mail. Yet of all the letters that arrived that day this small unassuming note about a speech I had made was the most important

"Dear Mr. Hilton:

"I have read your talk in the *Herald Tribune,* and I think it was wonderful. Especially that our faith in God was our only hope. You are very right and I think if everyone would fall down and pray we would have real peace. Sincerely yours, Daniel Paolucci.

"P.S. I am a boy of 12. May I please have an answer?"

If young Daniel knew what it did to the heart of a man to

find that a few of what he often feels are many repetitious words have fallen on listening ears, he would understand how grateful I was.

Automatically, I did the conventional thing. I wrote Daniel a grateful reply, enclosing a copy of the address he had liked. But I couldn't shake off his P.S.: "May I please have an answer?"

I reread the clipping in the *Herald Tribune:* "... in our struggle for freedom our greatest weapon will be our love of, and our faith in God." It dawned on me that something was lacking in that speech. Something that had been in Daniel's letter. Funny that I, who have known prayer and trusted the power of prayer all my life, should not have mentioned it.

It was on a train to Chicago that, mentally, I first saw Uncle Sam on his knees praying. Praying for what? Certainly not: "That God be on my side." Through two ghastly wars both sides made that prayer and it didn't get much peace even for the victor. Obviously, that hasn't worked. Daniel himself must have learned how foolish it would be to explain to his Algebra teacher how *he'd* like mathematics to work.

"That I be on God's side." That would be Uncle Sam's peace prayer.

Still fired with this concept when the train pulled into Chicago, I bought a daily paper. The first thing that caught my eye was a cartoon (opposite) entitled: "When Problems Overwhelm." Before a littered desk sat the figure of Uncle Sam, harassed by troubles. But he didn't look like the Uncle Sam I had visualized on the train: Strong, earnest, grounded on a rock of faith. Here sat the harassed old fellow. And from the wall an infinitely compassionate portrait of Abraham Lincoln spoke: "Have you tried prayer, Sam?"

To me it was the confirmation of my vision. Back in New York I talked it over with Dr. Norman Vincent Peale and my devoted friend, the late Fulton Oursler, both of whom encouraged me to proceed. In the spirit of humility and with loving advice a prayer took form.

Next came the idea for a pictorial presentation of the prayer—to be ready for publication in national magazines on Uncle Sam's birthday, July 4th, two months off.

Time was short. Where was the artist who could paint Uncle Sam? Paint him as he must be . . . not weak, not knocked to his knees, but freely, confidently, knowing how to do battle for peace.

Two of the greatest American artists were approached. They were enthusiastic, but their work schedule would not permit them to start immediately.

When a former secretary of mine, who had turned to painting, asked if she might try. I shrugged her off. Only a very great artist could do justice to the theme. But I wasn't reckoning with the power of prayer . . . one fruit of which is inspiration.

Several days later she handed me her work. I couldn't believe it. Here was the Uncle Sam I had seen on the train.

When I showed it to a Jesuit Father who knew her earlier works, he said simply, "She has painted better than she knows."

Within the first 5 days after "America on its Knees" appeared in national magazines, 5,000 people had written for 27,000 copies. Among them were hundreds of letters from children and teen-agers.

That was just the beginning of the snowball. Since then we have distributed 300,000 copies throughout the world. . . .

Here was the idea and how it grew. And I sat there that morning, in the Mayflower Hotel, seeing this event—the President, the Cabinet, Uncle Sam praying at the start of a new administration.

"Prayer today is a necessity," President Eisenhower stated when he arose to speak. "We know that our prayers may be imperfect . . . We are imperfect human beings. But if we can make the effort, then there is something that ties us all together."

Just prior to this I greeted the assemblage as proud host and then read the Uncle Sam prayer . . . The President of the United States, the Vice President, Cabinet, Justices, diplomats, top American leaders listened to the words below, which had been inspired by 12-year-old Daniel Paolucci . . .

OUR FATHER IN HEAVEN:

We pray that You save us from ourselves.

The world that You have made for us, to live in peace, we have made into an armed camp. We live in fear of war to come.

We are afraid of "the terror that flies by night, and the arrow that flies by day, the pestilence that walks in darkness and the destruction that wastes at noon-day."

We have turned from You to go our selfish way. We have broken Your commandments and denied Your truth. We have left Your altars to serve the false gods of money and pleasure and power. Forgive us and help us.

Now, darkness gathers around us and we are confused in all our counsels. Losing faith in You, we lose faith in ourselves.

Inspire us with wisdom, all of us, of every color, race and creed, to use our wealth, our strength, to help our brother, instead of destroying him.

Help us to do Your will as it is done in heaven and to be worthy of Your promise of peace on earth.

Fill us with new faith, new strength, and new courage, that we may win the battle for peace.

Be swift to save us, dear God, before the darkness falls.

Illustration, Uncle Sam at prayer, see page 201

THE STORY OF
KATHY FISCUS

by **ELAINE ST. JOHNS**

> *For days people throughout the world waited the result of a life-and-death drama outside of Los Angeles.*

THE TERSE VOICE of my city editor came over the phone, waking me from a deep sleep. "A little girl has fallen into a well." He ripped out the location of the accident and wound up with: "Get up there quick."

So I left my small daughter, tucked safely between white sheets, and drove across the dark city of Los Angeles to San Marino. It was more than 48 hours later before I kicked off muddy shoes in the city room of the *Los Angeles Mirror* and faced my typewriter.

I had all the facts, yet I had a stubborn feeling that something else was there—had been seen—but I couldn't find it in my notes. Then I made the newspaperman's prayer: "God, give me the vision to see what had actually happened. Give me the wisdom to report it accurately."

For two hours nothing came. It is hard to clear a vision that is blinded by human emotion and tears . . .

At 4:45 on a Friday afternoon in April 1949, a laughing little three-year-old child was playing with her small friends in a grassy vacant lot beside her home. Suddenly she disappeared; she had fallen into a long-abandoned well. Fifteen minutes later her mother called the police and reported that her daughter was wedged in the rusty old shaft. Half an hour later firemen were pumping oxygen into the small dark opening. At the end of an hour efforts to raise Kathy with a rope failed and at six o'clock power equipment began digging a parallel hole.

During this brief time the girl called back bravely to the familiar world above her. She answered those she loved, always with courage. "Yes, I'm all right." She wanted to please.

"Will you try to grab hold of the rope, Kathy?"

"I am, *I am!*" Then her voice ceased, but she had spoken long enough to convince those above her that she was unhurt.

By the time I reached the lot it was no longer vacant. Under a blaze of lights, men and machines had begun to battle with Mother Earth. Men by the hundreds began to volunteer their help. Circus midgets, living in the vicinity arrived, and risked being lowered by their feet into the crumbling old shaft . . . there were Boy Scouts, acrobats, engineers, firemen.

By daybreak people throughout the world were invisible spectators. Newspapers, radio and television put aside war and international news to headline the story of a rescue attempt.

Bill Yancey, 38-year-old contractor, was one of the Navy's underwater demolition men who cleared the water of mines on the fortified beaches long before the first troops attempted landing. Bill was the first man into the rescue shaft, the last man out. At one stretch he sweated five back-breaking feet of earth out of that hole in an hour and a half.

An ex-sand hogger and boilermaker left his home in the San Fernando Valley the minute he heard of the accident. In spite of the stabbing pain of a hernia this man, Whitey Blickensderfer, stayed at his dangerous job beneath the ground until he collapsed and was taken to the hospital.

The father of five children, 25-year-old Clyde Harp, sneaked out of his own home to volunteer his help, although he had not done any deep excavation work for a long time. "I didn't want to worry my wife," he said, "but I have five good reasons at home for lending a hand at the digging."

Seldom had so much prayer power been focused on one person and on one rescue. Exhausted, gray-faced men continued their dangerous work against water, sand and cascades of rock. And what was happening around the world?

Men on a lonely watch on a ship far at sea followed the progress and took up a collection. Hard coal miners in Denver had offered their help. A neighbor brought a chocolate cake, the only offering she could think of, to the family. One man bought over 700 gallons of hot coffee and stacks of doughnuts.

Meanwhile, sitting side by side, in a parked car during most of these frantic operations were the girl's white-faced mother and father. Beneath the giant machines and rigging, the bright lights, the microphone booming directions lay a tiny figure whom none of these gallant rescuers had ever seen. Was all well with her? Was there water where she lay? Did she still know moments of consciousness and fear?

Fifty-three hours following the accident, after a total expenditure of a quarter of a million dollars—Bill Yancey was lowered into the rescue shaft on a bucket fastened to the end of a cable, while the world above waited.

Then the answer came up. Men had lost. Kathy Fiscus, a little girl whom the whole world came to know, was dead, gone shortly after she last spoke. Those were the facts I had to report.

But not the end of the story. I knew there was something that would explain the frantic, futile fight.

I looked around the city room. There were the usual reports coming in: wars, strikes, families in trouble, racial problems.

And suddenly I saw the contrast.

There on the vacant lot, in San Marino, the whole world had united, for a few hours, over the life of one child.

Men had not lost. A little girl got people to loving one another. No distinction of color, race or creed, rich or poor, rose to mar the efforts of people who fought to save one made in His image.

That was the story. That was the miracle of Kathy Fiscus.

Illustration, Kathy Fiscus, see page 201

A CANDLE FOR POPSY

by **HERBERT KAMM**

*A father and son have a memorable experience in
a Church of another faith.*

WE STOOD uncertainly at Fiftieth Street on Fifth Avenue, my
son's arm tight around my thigh, as we threaded through the
shopping hordes who seemed to move in accelerated frenzy on
this last Saturday before Christmas.

Larry's nose was tipped with the crimson of winter when he
looked up at me, and the wind had painted high spots of color
on his cheeks. I asked if he wanted hot chocolate, but he shook
his head and vetoed Radio City as well.

Then, while I searched for another suggestion, he tugged at
my arm, and pointed at the spires of St. Patrick's Cathedral. His
hand fumbled for mine and gripped it tightly through his fur-
lined mittens.

"Gee, Dad," he said.

We had seen the animated window displays this rich afternoon. We had seen the toys in the stores, and the giant evergreen
in Rockefeller Plaza, and the confusingly numerous Santa
Clauses on the street corners.

He had laughed, and danced, and sung out with delight at all
this. Now he was awed. He was only six, but he had called me
Dad from the time he had brushed the awkward remnants of
baby talk out of his speech. It was never Daddy, but Dad—as if
he were urging maturity upon himself.

"Let's go inside, Dad," he said.

I hesitated for a reason that is not easy to explain. After all, we
were Jews, and—

"Can't we go inside, Dad?" He spoke breathlessly, as do children who are about to trespass on the secrets of a long-empty house.

"Sure," I said. "Sure we can go inside."

We picked an opening through the thickening throng—it was late afternoon now—and started slowly up the shallow steps. Then suddenly I remembered, and I bent over and reminded him to remove his hat when we entered.

"This is different than in *shul*," I said. "You always take your hat off in a Christian church."

We walked through the massive doors, and as we passed into the shadows, he removed his brown Eton cap and choked it into his coat pocket.

We tiptoed up the center aisle. His head was rigid, but I could see his eyes steal to the right and to the left, scanning the people kneeling in prayer.

He might have been just a little frightened at first—until his eyes beheld the main altar. His hand pressed deeper into mine.

"Golly, Dad."

We took a few more steps, and now we were abreast of the front pew. As we stood there, our vision fell into focus with the soft lights. Before us, on the high altar, was the image of Jesus.

"Dad, who is that?" His gaze was unmoved.

"Jesus," I said. "That's Jesus, Son."

He was silent for a moment. "Dad, who was Jesus?"

I closed my eyes for a moment, thinking as hard as I ever had, for, Jew or Gentile, you want to give your son the right answer when he asks that kind of question.

"We of the Jewish faith," I said, "believe that Jesus was a prophet."

He nodded.

"The Christian people believe that Jesus was more than a learned man. They believe, too, that He was—and is—the son of God."

"It's beautiful, Dad," he said, still looking at the statue.

I waited until his hand relaxed its grip on mine and then motioned him toward the pew.

He sat down rigidly and folded his hands between his knees. We sat for what seemed a long time, neither of us saying anything. Then he saw the rows of votive lights.

"What are they for?"

"I think," I said with some uncertainty, "that they are lighted in memory of people who have died."

He nodded and looked back at them, the candles flickering in the recesses on either side of the great cathedral and to the right and left of the altar.

He drew me toward him again, his expression eager.

"I want to light one for Popsy," he said.

Popsy was my father. He had died the previous April—eons ago in the life of a child—but Larry hadn't forgotten.

A candle for Popsy . . . in St. Patrick's Cathedral . . . and almost on the eve of Christmas.

"You bet you can light a candle for Popsy," I said.

We sidled through the pew and tiptoed around to an alcove where a medley of candles burned brightly in white glasses.

I reached for a taper, but he pulled my arm down.

"Please, Dad," he said. "The ones in the red glasses."

He walked ahead of me to a tray of lights and stood stiffly before it. His hand came up slowly, and he drew a fresh taper from the receptacle below the first row of lights.

He touched it to one of the burning candles, then to an unlighted one. He watched the flame rise to full height, replaced the taper and smiled up at me.

"For Popsy," he said.

I nodded. "For Popsy," I said.

We watched teardrops of wax form in the glass, turned and walked hand in hand down the aisle and out into the street.

Illustration, Herbert Kamm and son Larry, see page 200

WHAT'S THE REAL SCORE?

by DAN TOWLER

*One of the best halfbacks in professional football
wants, more than anything else, to be a minister
some day. Before playing football, here are the questions Don Towler had to answer for himself.*

SCOUTS OF THE Los Angeles Rams first saw me playing college
football at Washington and Jefferson College. After graduation
I was invited to their 1950 summer training camp to compete
for a job on the famous Ram team against such stars as Bob
Waterfield, Dick Hoerner, Glenn Davis, Elroy Hirsch and
Norm Van Brocklin.

I believed I had the physical ability, but realized my need for
help and guidance to make the grade. Half-scared, I turned to a
source of strength that has never failed me—prayer. Prayer, to
me, has always been personal communication with God.

At the Ram training camp I spent from thirty to forty-five
minutes each day in a devotional period which consisted of
prayer, reading the Bible and straightening out my viewpoints.
I had to answer, for myself, certain questions.

Why had I gone into sports?

I had done it to keep the body, that holds my soul, in a fine,
workable condition. It is the instrument God gives us to live one
lifetime in. He does not mean for it to be neglected. No athlete
is ignorant of the hard way of strict self-discipline, self-mastery,
self-control and the curbing of appetites.

What was my life goal?

The career of a professional athlete, to a dedicated person, can
be as great a calling as is medicine, teaching, or the ministry. For

a few years, then, it would be that for me. But my life goal is to enter the ministry.   •

I have been a divinity student now for several years, taking my training during the months I'm not playing football. They call me "Deacon Dan," which is all right with me. I have been interested in the church ever since I can remember. As a toddler I began attending services, joined the First Baptist Church of Donora, Pennsylvania, at the age of eight. I worked in our Baptist Training Union as a youth, and, for a long time, was an integral part of a Junior Prayer Group. In such a group I found a medium for a working faith in God and association with my fellow men.

Would any personal or financial success that I might obtain in football hurt my future ministry? Long hours of meditation and the counsel of others helped me see that money and success are not sinful in themselves. Only if misused, or overstressed, are they destructive to morals and character and lead one away from God.

And there was also the challenge that a minister on the football field could be effective for God.

All this cleared my outlook and lessened my tension. I wanted to make good. I could pray for such success with a clear heart.

Before each exhibition game that summer, and later before the league games, I continued to offer private prayers for the team. Then the thought occurred to me, how much better it would be if the whole team would pray together, before each game. I finally got up enough courage to ask Joe Stydahar, our Coach at the time.

"Coach, would you think it out of order on my part to suggest that the team unite in prayer before each game?" I said nervously.

Coach Stydahar was for the idea. Although it was already the middle of the season, he saw that a few moments were set aside before each remaining game, in which period we could acknowledge the presence of God and ask for His guidance and strength.

The following season we continued to make this prayer a regular part of the Ram's pre-game preparations. The crux of this prayer is for one to "pray as though everything depended on God and then go out on the field and play as though everything depended on you."

Not that our victories come about because of the prayer sessions. God doesn't play favorites that way. But I am convinced that the mental attitude developed by a player before a game contributes greatly to the spirit, and to the success, of himself and the team as a whole.

Illustration, Dan Towler, see page 201

TEN MEN AND A PRAYER

by **FRED SCHILLER**

*Where could these grizzled infantrymen find the
tenth man? A story that will be told and retold
wherever veterans of World War II meet.*

I was a buck private attached to Company C of the 846 Signal
Photo Battalion. Sitting next to me in the station waiting room
was a lieutenant of the much-decorated Third Infantry Division
just back from European combat. It was early 1945.

When we started casual talk, I discovered that his name was
McBride and that he was going home to Indiana on furlough.
He told one experience with moving simplicity, then left to
catch his train. His story is still vivid in my mind, even after
seven years, that I have an almost irresistible compulsion to
relate it . . .

Italian hill "46" was finally abandoned on orders one bleak
spring day back in 1944. As the weary GIs filed back towards
the little Italian town of San Pietro, behind which American
artillery answered the enemy, Sergeant Frazer began counting
the costs of their mission.

"How many men left in your squad, Murphy?"

"Four, countin' myself."

Frazer then moved down the thin line of troops towards Max
Halpern, a grizzled, flint-eyed Corporal, who carried a light
machine gun cradled in his arm like a baby.

"Rosy got his right after the jump," said the Corporal. "Best
squad leader I ever had." "Rosy" was Sergeant Rosenberg.

The remnants of the platoon then moved into the shattered
village. The rest of their company had gathered beside a small
church with only three walls and half roof left. The section

leaders were conferring with Lieutenant McBride beside the torn wall of the church.

"We'll wait here till the battalion assembles," said the officer. "Have your men ready to move out again in half an hour."

Corporal Halpern signaled his men to relax and, still cradling the machine gun, walked into the cool shadows inside the church. He didn't want to talk to anybody just then; he was feeling too keenly about his buddy, "Rosy," who had touched off the mine explosion that had cleared the way for the rest of the squad's advance.

Halpern looked wearily around the quiet, littered pews. But the cross above the altar remained in place and in the aisle, in front of the pews, knocked from its pedestal by the concussion of shell fire, standing upright, stood a statue of Christ. Glass and plaster fragments were everywhere, even on the altar and chancel floor.

For the first time in three days the knots inside Halpern began to loosen. He realized how tired he was. And the loss of a buddy overwhelmed him. Corporal Halpern lifted his eyes toward the altar and the sky above the shattered roof.

"Oh, God," he thought, "why—"

Suddenly Halpern laid his machine gun in a corner and walked outside to Lieutenant McBride.

"Lieutenant, while we're waiting, I want to round up ten fellows of our faith and say a prayer for Sergeant Rosenberg."

"Sure, Corporal. But why ten?"

"It's the Jewish prayer, 'Minjeh.' According to Hebrew ritual it requires ten Hebrews."

The Corporal went off up the street among the rubble heaps and the little groups of men. When he returned, some minutes later, with a group of fellow GIs, the lieutenant was standing inside the church.

"Found them okay, Corporal?"

"No," said Halpern, "I'm short one man. Been through the whole battalion, but the rest are either killed or wounded. Don't know what I can do without the tenth either." The Corporal looked from his friends to the lieutenant.

"I don't think the Almighty would mind too much if one were absent," said Lt. McBride.

Corporal Halpern glanced toward the altar of the church and then up through the torn roof.

"I'll manage, Lieutenant," he said. "Come on fellows." The Corporal led the way down the church aisle and in silence arranged the eight men and himself in a circle before the chancel.

The lieutenant, at the back of the church, uncovered his head in reverence and then looked in surprise as he saw what Halpern was doing.

The Corporal gently lifted the statue of Christ and placed it in the circle between two of his buddies.

"Jesus was a Jew," he said softly. "He makes us ten."

Then he took out a little prayer book. "Repeat after me," he said to the quiet circle of his Jewish comrades. The prayer of "Minjeh" rose solemnly . . . Sergeant Rosenberg would not be forgotten.

Illustration, Fred Schiller, see page 200

PAGE 255

PAGE 263

SPECIALISTS

IN OVERCOMING

OBSTACLES

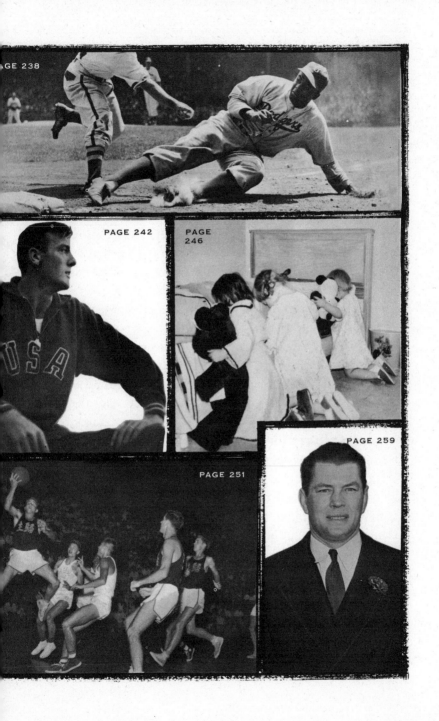

PAGE 238

PAGE 242

PAGE 246

PAGE 251

PAGE 259

TROUBLE AHEAD
NEEDN'T BOTHER YOU

by **JACKIE ROBINSON**

> *Jackie Robinson, Brooklyn Dodgers baseball star,
> and Branch Rickey changed baseball history. But
> the day they decided on this action, they knew what
> they were facing, and what help they'd need.*

I'LL NEVER FORGET the day Branch Rickey, former President of
the Brooklyn Dodgers, asked me to join his baseball organization. I would be the first Negro to play in organized baseball—
that is, if I were good enough to make the grade.

Mr. Rickey's office was large and simply furnished. There
were four framed pictures on the wall. One was a Kodachrome
snapshot of Leo Durocher, the field manager of the Dodgers,
and now manager of the New York Giants. Another was a
portrait of the late Charlie Barrett, one of the greatest scouts in
the game. A third was of General Chennault. And the fourth
and largest smiled down on me with calm reassurance, the
portrait of the sad, trusting Abraham Lincoln who had pleaded
for malice toward none. . . .

This was the never-to-be-forgotten day when our Marines
landed on the soil of Japan, August 29, 1945. It was a hot day,
with venetian blinds shutting out the sun, and the Brooklyn
clamor of Montague Street mingled with the noisy traffic around
Borough Hall.

From behind his desk the big, powerful, bushy-browed
Branch Rickey, who seemed a combination of father and boss,
mapped out to me his daring strategy to break the color line in
major league baseball.

I was excited at the opportunity. It was a tremendous challenge. But was I good enough?

238

"Mr. Rickey," I said, "it sounds like a dream come true—not only for me but for my race. For seventy years there has been racial exclusion in big league baseball. There will be trouble ahead—for you, for me, for my people, and for baseball."

"Trouble ahead," Rickey rolled the phrase over his lips as though he liked the sound. "You know, Jackie, I was a small boy when I took my first train ride. On the same train was an old couple, also riding for the first time. We were going through the Rocky Mountains. The old man sitting by the window looked forward and said to his wife, 'Trouble ahead, Ma! We're high up over a precipice and we're gonna run right off.'

"To my boyish ears the noise of the wheels repeated 'Trouble-a-head-trouble-ahead. . . .' I never hear train wheels to this day but what I think of this. But our train course bent into a tunnel right after the old man spoke, and we came out on the other side of the mountain. That's the way it is with most trouble ahead in this world, Jackie—if we use the common sense and courage God gave us. But you've got to study the hazards and build wisely."

I've never forgotten that little story. It helped me through many of the rough moments I was to face in the future. I signed my contract that day with a humble feeling of great responsibility. I prayed that I would be equal to the test.

"God is with us in this, Jackie," Mr. Rickey said quietly. "You know your Bible. It's good, simple Christianity for us to face realities and to recognize what we're up against. We can't go out and preach and crusade and bust our heads against a wall. We've got to fight out our problems together with tact and common sense."

To give me experience and seasoning, Mr. Rickey sent me the first year to play with the Montreal Royals, a farm club for the Brooklyn organization. I was the cause of trouble from the start—but we expected it. Pre-season exhibition games were canceled because of "mixed athletes," although the official reason was always different.

Some of my teammates may have resented me. If so, I didn't blame them. They had problems enough playing ball without being a part of a racial issue. I tried hard not to develop "rabbit ears," a malady picked up by all athletes who are sensitive to abuse and criticism shouted from the fans.

One of my top thrills was my opening game for Montreal at Jersey City. The pressure was on and I was very nervous. But during that contest I slapped out four hits, including a home run. I couldn't have dreamed up a better start.

But as the season began to unroll game after game, my playing grew erratic. I was trying too hard. I knew I had to keep my temper bridled at every turn. Guarding so carefully against outbursts can put a damper on one's competitive spirit.

Every athlete at some time or other likes "to blow his top." It seldom does any harm and acts like a safety valve. A hitter in a slump may drive the ball deep to the infield, then leg it to first, sure that he has beaten the throw. The umpire calls him out. With this the frustrated athlete jerks off his cap, slams it on the ground and thunders all his pent-up irritations at the umpire. The crowd roars its approval or dislike depending on whether the player is on the home or visiting team. The umpire merely turns his back, and the ball player, after giving vent to his unhappiness, trots back to the bench feeling much better. It's all a part of the game.

But I didn't dare let loose this way. Many would have dubbed me a "hothead" and point to my outburst as a reason why Negroes should not play in organized baseball. This was one of the hardest problems I had to face.

As the season rolled along, however, the players became accustomed to me. My play improved. When the season ended, Montreal had won the Junior World Series. I admit proudly to winning the batting championship of the league with an average of .349.

On April 10, 1947 Branch Rickey made the announcement that gave me my greatest thrill. I was to join the Brooklyn Dodgers and become the first Negro to compete in the major leagues.

It was Montreal all over again, but this time the pressure was much greater, the competition keener, and the stakes tremendous. It wasn't a question so much of a Negro athlete making good as a big leaguer, but whether the whole racial question would be advanced or retarded.

Again I faced the same problems. An opposing player drove a hard grounder to the infield. When he crossed first base his spikes bit painfully into my foot. Accident or deliberate? Who can tell? But the first reaction of a competitive ball player is to double up fists and lash out. I saw a blinding red. It took every bit of my discipline to bridle my temper. But when my teammates rushed to my support in white hot anger, it gave me the warmest feeling I've ever felt. At that moment I belonged.

That year the Dodgers won the pennant. I was thrilled to know that my efforts were considered an important factor in winning. But I also cherished another triumph. Baseball as a whole had come to accept the Negro. Since then a number of Negros, including Larry Doby, Monte Irvin, Henry Thompson, Willie Mays—and Don Newcomb, Roy Campenella and Junior Gilliam on the Dodgers—have developed into Major League stars. To make the grade they simply had to have the ability. As Mr. Rickey says, a champion is a champion in America, black or white.

Illustration, Jackie Robinson sliding into third base, see page 237

WHAT KIND OF
TEAM HAVE WE?

by **BOB MATHIAS**

> *One of America's greatest athletes had anemia as a*
> *boy and sat on the sidelines watching others play*
> *games. Bob Mathias, who rose spectacularly above*
> *this handicap, tells here why young people today are*
> *no "beat generation."*

JUDGING FROM some of the things we hear and read today, our younger generation is in a bad way.

One article, for example, labeled us the "beat generation." You would think we majored in driving cars like maniacs, smoking marijuana and scoffing at good morals.

No one denies there are irresponsible kids in "hopped up" cars. But the hot rod drivers *I've* known have been mostly pretty earnest lads who regarded themselves as architects of ideas which they made happen on old cars. The boys who run the police blockades, aren't socially acceptable among the ones I've met who spend hours tinkering over an engine.

Twice I've known boys who experimented with marijuana. One was a college lad who thought he was being "smart." Instead, he just bored everyone. The other was a high school boy. He waited until he had quite an audience including some of the most attractive girls in school. Then he gave the big pitch about his "weed."

"So what?" said one of the girls. "That doesn't take any brains or courage. *Anyone* can do that."

To the guy who tries to attract attention by flagrant conduct, the average girl still says, "so what?" As one girl told a fellow I know, "I don't want to have to crawl on my stomach to look up to the man I marry."

A recent survey stated that youth, as a whole, lacks any real faith and has a lusterless attack on life.

This survey concluded that there was little indication that we were willing "to risk the cost which may be involved in doing new things, going to new places, venturing into new vocations, or trying out a new idea."

If that's the sort of team we are, the future is already lost. A team with such spirit wouldn't win many games and would be an awfully hard one to play on. I've been in some of the scrimmages in high schools and colleges around the country, however, and come up with an entirely different picture.

Take a fellow we'll call George since he wants no publicity. A few years ago George was a football hero. Easy going, popular, he graduated straight into the Service. He did all right there too, and came back to land an excellent job in one of San Francisco's oldest industries. Last year he had two promotions and was on his way to the top. He has a lovely wife and is expecting his first child. Could any man ask more in the way of a secure, riskless future?

Last week George announced that he was quitting his job. "By the time I become a father I'll be a Stanford law student," he said.

Why? George's answer is simple.

"I got the feeling I wasn't doing anything. That there's a lot to be done." Law, he felt, was where he could make his best contribution.

Was his young bride willing to exchange the life of an executive's wife, with three bedrooms and two baths, to living in cramped quarters and keeping the baby quiet while her husband studied 55 to 60 hours weekly?

"George has too much on the ball to settle in a rut even if it's lined with mink," she replied.

Another young man I know courted his girl all through his

pre-med course and won her hand while he still had five years
of school left. Her father almost forbade the event when his prospective son-in-law refused to give up his 18-hour-a-day grind.
The boy couldn't see any future for their marriage if he took
a 9-5 job in his father-in-law's business just so daughter could
live as comfortably as she'd always lived.

Today this young bride is occupying a little converted garage
at the edge of the golf course.

It's hard to believe that this country is filled with immoral
teen clubs and law-defying young men when so few of us ever
encounter them. Certainly they are a minority.

I get hundreds of letters today from kids in high school and
junior high. There's nothing "beat" about them either. They
want to know about health habits. Training rules. They are
also aware that the spirit behind the effort is just as important as
physical fitness.

"I'm out for track and I'm not very good at it," one high school
boy wrote. "I get kidded quite a bit by the gang. Should I stick?"

He could take the kidding; but he didn't want to be a quitter
to himself. He wasn't worried about conformity and he wasn't
too worried about winning. He was willing to go along as an
"also-ran" if it was making a better man of him.

I wrote him to stick, remembering that one guy can run fast,
another can't. But if he tried to do his best at everything he
started, he'd soon find something he could do better than anyone else. This was my experience.

I grew up in a normal household in Tulare, California—three
boys, one girl. My dad was a model of self-discipline, a hard-
working doctor, while my mother always has been the busiest
woman I know. Small and vivacious, she managed all our
laundry, cooking, cleaning and had energy left over. She had
time for civic activities in town, and yet somewhere along the
line she became a walking record-book of sports information.

We were always throwing balls or running races. As mother says, "It seemed like there was always a track meet going on in our backyard. Ours was one home that never had a garden— just a garden of kids."

While Dad made the athletic equipment in our garage available to the whole neighborhood, it was mother who made sure it was all put back. We kids alternated with the dish washing and I remember that, as a Cub Scout, my idea of a good deed was to wash them without making a big fuss.

Then there was the time I had anemia. I can remember taking refuge in a big tree outside our house and watching the other guys play rugged games. I used to dream about playing with them, and yearn for the secrets of victory. Thanks to this illness, I discovered early the importance of proper rest and good eating habits. Learning how to relax in the middle of the day helped me a great deal during both Olympics.

It was my wife, Melba, who startled me before we were married with the idea that a lot of responsibility went with my athletic awards. "Those letters you get from kids are cutting out your future for you," she said.

That was pretty hard to figure at first. The things I do don't seem very great. If there is some special secret to athletic victory I don't know it. From what I've seen of champions, their success is an open book, easy to read, hard to apply: good health habits, moderation, discipline, and so forth. Most important, an athlete needs both faith in himself and faith in a higher Power.

The growing enthusiasm of youth for religion is reason in itself why we're no "beat generation." We do have faith in the future. We could be greatly strengthened by some faith in us.

Illustration, Bob Mathias, see page 237

THE RUN-AWAY

by AMELIA ANTHONY

"I hate God," said the defiant girl. The founder of Girlstown studied her rebel helplessly, wondering how she could handle her toughest case.

THE DISTRESSED voices in the corridor awoke me. Then came the knock on my door.

"Mama! Myrna is running away! Mama!"

Putting on my robe, I looked at my watch. It was 2 A.M. Standing at the door were three of my girls, young faces clouded with anxiety.

"Myrna's packing," Ellen said. "She says she doesn't want to stay here anymore."

"All right, dear," I said. "Go back to your rooms. I'll talk to Myrna."

Dressing, I realized that "talk" was about all I could do with Myrna. We could not prevent her from running away. When Girlstown was established in 1949, I wanted it to be a true home, so there were no fences or barriers. Only the quality of love and sense of belonging would keep Myrna and others from leaving.

But love had seemed a weak weapon against Myrna. Since the day three weeks before, when juvenile authorities had turned her over to me, she had rebuffed my every attempt to get close to her. Myrna seemed hardened at fifteen in a way that would have been pitiful in a mature woman.

She had parents but they neglected her. She was not eligible for an orphanage. Since she had done nothing wrong, there was no need to send her to a detention institution. Myrna had no suitable relatives. No one wanted her.

But I did. For youngsters like her I had founded Girlstown. I remembered asking Myrna when we met: "Would you like to live with us in a real house on the range?"

She just shrugged, her eyes hostile.

Other girls had actually wept after their first day at the farm, deeply touched by their first adventure with kindness and love, wide-eyed at the ranch house, barns, chicken yards and animals. There were no tears or wonder in Myrna's eyes.

That first night she sat alone in the living room, apart from the others, ignoring our games and songs, staring coldly ahead while the rest of the girls bowed their heads for night-prayers.

I felt Myrna was sizing us up, figuring us out, and I believed that after a day or so she would realize that we were being sincere and honest with her, and then she would become one of us.

But I was wrong. Soon I began to fear that I was about to suffer my first failure.

One day 12-year-old Susan accidentally spilled something on Myrna's dress. Whirling Susan around by the shoulder, Myrna blasted her with a shocking outburst. Immediately, I took Myrna to my office and assured her firmly that I would not tolerate such language.

She studied me coolly and then said: "This place is worse than a jail."

That night, as I had done often before, I told my daughters: "Our home here has a foundation made of faith, walls which are love and a ceiling which is truth." A look of amused contempt came upon Myrna's face, and I was thankful the others hadn't seen it.

All the girls loved to cook, plan menus, budget kitchen expenses, make their own clothes—even milk the cows and tend the cattle. By performing these various duties, the girls feel they earn the $1 a week allowance we give each one. Furthermore the chores train them to be good housewives and mothers, useful citizens and active Christians. But Myrna showed no interest in any of these activities.

One day I overheard another girl say to her: "You don't appreciate anything around here, do you?"

"Why should I?" Myrna replied. "I didn't ask to come here and I don't have to stay."

And now she had decided to go.

I hurried to her room where she was packing her suitcase with grand flourishes. When she saw me, her taut face set in determined lines.

"You're leaving?" I asked.

"It looks like it," she said curtly.

The window was opened—obviously her escape. I helped her pack. "Ladies leave by the front door," I said and, picking up her suitcase, led her into the living room.

I opened the door and handed her the bag. "Good-bye, Myrna," I said. "I know that God will watch over you."

She looked up at me quickly, and for an instant her dark eyes filled with confusion. Then she clenched her teeth and walked off into the dark night. I watched her until she was out of sight. Defeated, I closed the door and went to my office.

Too crushed even for tears, I sat there, numbed by my first failure. And when words finally came to me, they were a prayer. I begged God to show me what I had done wrong, what to do next.

Girlstown had been my lifelong dream. As a social worker I had seen countless young girls who were unwanted, had nowhere to go and slipped off eventually into the darkness of serious delinquency. For years I searched for some way to protect them from that black future.

When enough money had been saved, I opened a small home for girls in Buffalo Gap, Texas. Four months later I received, by deeded gift, surface rights to a 1,425-acre property nine miles south of Whiteface, Texas. The buildings we constructed became Girlstown, U.S.A. We have made it as homelike as possible, and accepted full responsibility for girls of all ages and the duty of preparing them for constructive womanhood. The balance of our family here comprises 22 adult staff members.

As my legal wards, the girls are my daughters, but I know they will consider me their mother only if I give them the love, attention and guidance a mother should. That is what I have tried to do.

Myrna had been the fifty-third girl to arrive. And the first to run away . . .

The knock at the door was so light it almost escaped me. It was Myrna, uncertain but still defiant.

"I want to talk to you," she said, "but just for a few minutes. I'm not staying. But there's something I must know." Her voice trembled, but she tried to keep the bitterness in it.

"Why did you say God would watch over me?" she demanded.

"Because He will," I said.

"He never has," she said. "Why should He start now? He's left me alone all these years. Why should He suddenly care for me? I don't care for Him. I hate Him!"

"No you don't!" I said, suddenly realizing her terrible loneliness and hunger for the love her unfortunate childhood forced her to reject. "God has cared for you in many ways."

"Like what?" she challenged. "Such as giving me a prostitute for a mother and a drunkard for a father? Like giving me a murderer for a grandfather and a bootlegger for an uncle? Like putting me in the streets so the police can pick me up? Like giving me a life that can only make me a prostitute like my mother? Well, if that's how God has cared for me, I might as well get started now!"

The words tumbled through the wall of hate she had built for herself. She was shaking and I wanted to take her into my arms.

"God hasn't given you those things," I said. "He couldn't because they're evil. If you think you have this same kind of life ahead of you, it's only because you're making the mistake your family made: you won't let yourself love God. And you can't be aware of His love until you do."

"What has God done to show me that He wants my love?" she said.

"He has brought you back here."

She stood there, and her eyes mirrored the conflict between what the hard years had taught her and what she now suddenly wanted.

Abruptly, the sobs came. And she was in my arms.

The next day, Myrna was so different the other girls were slightly reticent.

But I kept hoping for something more. That moment came on a Sunday morning.

Accompanying other girls, Myrna had joined a congregation whose people wanted to build a new church. This Sunday, the pastor suggested that men of the congregation contribute a portion of their salaries to meet remaining expenses. Myrna was suddenly on her feet.

"Most of you know I'm from Girlstown. I have my dollar a week allowance I can give. But I want to do something more. I want to work to earn money for the new church."

Other girls joined her. At Girlstown, they baked pies and cakes and sold them. In one week, they made $60. Their example inspired the rest of the congregation, and everyone did something special to raise the necessary funds.

Weeks later, I saw Myrna and five other girls kneel at the church altar and, through baptism, accept their responsibilities as Christians. Afterwards, Myrna came to me.

"You've always said you've built Girlstown on a foundation of faith," she said. "Well, I think everything must be built that way, if it's to endure."

Illustration, Prayer time at Girls Town, see page 237

VENTURE FOR VICTORY

by **DONALD G. ODLE**

> *Basketball players as ambassadors! Here are ex-*
> *cerpts from the diary of the coach who directed this*
> *unique mission. Donald Odle is Athletic Director*
> *and Basketball Coach at Taylor University in Up-*
> *land, Indiana.*

The beginnings: (Jan. 1952) A long distance call from Formosa. "This is Dick Hillis . . . can you gather together some of your basketball players and come over here next month?"

I told Dick the boys couldn't leave their books in February, but that we would come in the summer. Hillis (a Christian missionary representing an evangelical organization called Oriental Crusades) said it would be too hot, but we decided to try it any-way.

Boys were picked on a competitive basis on following points in order of importance: (1) Strength of religious experience and convictions. (2) Speaking ability on above. (3) Musical ability—singing—instruments. (4) Basketball ability.

We're off: The boys traveled light . . . basketball equipment, Bibles, hymn books and a message. Basketball secondary to bringing message of Christ to Far Eastern neighbors as an answer to Communism. We called it "Venture For Victory."

This was the strategy: between halves of each game, the players would hold a service, then talk personally with all who remained after game. Those interested would be enrolled in a Bible course provided by Oriental Crusades.

We raised our own finances, planned the tour with help of Hillis and Youth for Christ. It often was rugged going. The boys slept on floors, ate what and when they could; they encountered

riots, a typhoon, rats, a plague. They played basketball on baseball fields, in bombed-out buildings, in huge stadiums, in air-
plane hangars, in cleared out area of a lumber camp, in the
middle of a jungle. They often played two games a day, sometimes three, under the tropical sun. Countries visited included
Hawaii, Philippines, Formosa, Korea, Japan, China.

Formosa: Madame Chiang Kai-shek approved the original
idea to bring American athletic teams to Formosa to help morale
in Chinese Army camps, and her prayer group acted as official
hostesses.

We played at the Refugee Camp. To make drinking water
drinkable we put Alka Seltzer in it. At first practice I noticed
that Chinese boys were fascinated by hair on legs of Americans.
They have none on their own limbs.

It was very hot, but the boys never stopped hustling. Between
halves is our big opportunity. Statements, readings and singing
must be sharp and to the point.

Humor: The pace is rough; sense of humor paramount. Floyd
"Moose" Habick, 6 ft. 5 in. center, provided most of the laughs.
He was like a bull in a china shop. If we heard something break,
someone would cry, "Moose's done it again." There was another
boy named Bear. Moose would go around saying, "Bear, are
you there?" and Bear would come right back, "Moose, are you
loose?"

Our first attempt at humor before Orientals fell flat until we
started to talk about our big feet, big noses, etc. At the start
of his talk, Moose would say, "I have two distinctions. I am
the tallest member of the team. I am also the ugliest."

When we left Honolulu, the native girls gave us leis of flowers,
all except Moose. Being such a big eater, he was presented a
wreath of hot dogs and mustard. Moose was quite grateful; on
the plane he got the hostess to cook six of the franks. How we
loved Moose—and needed him. And the team kept a sense of

humor whether eating with chopsticks or sleeping in beds with frogs.

The Philippines: We held church services, spoke in high schools, Army camps, colleges, averaging two games and five services a day on the various islands. We learned that some Filipinos believe the way to find forgiveness of sins is to be beaten on the back until the blood runs.

A crowd of 8000 showed up for the game. Between halves we stressed that Christ forgives us of sin and releases us for more effective living. What are the results of meetings like this? Who can judge? We speak from sincerity and conviction. No one but God can keep accurate books. Yet we overheard such statements as this from a native soldier, "God, forgive me for my sins." Once a group of natives, with tears in their eyes, gave up clay idols they had worshipped for years.

Typhoon and Plague: The crossing from Kinmen to the island of Taipai by plane was a beaut. The Island was one mile from Communist territory and had once been shelled. In our planes were holes for guns in case of air attack. Then a typhoon struck and we thought it was the end. As the plane bounced all over the sky, we were bruised and airsick. Before landing, the pilot said, "No one is to leave the plane." While taxiing up, we could see ambulances, police. What was wrong? Had the Communists taken over? Or did local police think we were Communists?

The police boarded the plane and pulled their guns—spray guns. We were fumigated thoroughly. "You have come from an area of bubonic plague," said the officer, "and we're taking no chances."

Riot: There were 9000 people on Taipai when we started the game. Some in the crowd were ugly, spat in the faces of the referees, began throwing bottles. The situation was very dangerous.

The manager of the stadium got a bright idea. "There are

Communists in the crowd," he shouted in the native tongue on a P.A. system. "They want to confuse the game." From then on, the silence was breathtaking. Communists were shot on sight in Taipai. No one wanted to risk this.

Hong Kong: Here we were in the middle of Communist influence. After beating their best team by 50 points, the Communist papers did not give the score, called us bad sports and sorry players. We called our team "Gua Jai" (for Christ) which they reported as "For America." Of course, we were for America. Actually, we had two purposes: (1) Christianity as a way of life. (2) Emphasize the freedoms we believe are worth fighting for. The language was often a barrier, but we always had translators wherever we went.

Conclusion: The boys, typical American kids, did themselves proud in the physical and spiritual give-and-take. They were a praying, yet fun-loving bunch. We won 79 consecutive games over one stretch, the only game we lost was to the Philippine Olympic quintet.

Despite all the resistance—superstition, language barriers, Communist tricks, difficult physical conditions—we reached a total of 500,000 people. Response especially good in Korea and Formosa. Fred Jarvis, U.N. Correspondent in Formosa, reported: "Venture for Victory has opened a new door in the field of evangelism. Without question, this group has left a testimony for Christ that will not soon be forgotten." We sincerely hope so.

Illustration, Basketball action in Far East, see page 237

LET NOT THY
LEFT HAND KNOW

by ROBERT CHRISTENBERRY

The transition from civilian-to-army-to-civilian sta-
tus has always been difficult. Bob Christenberry tells
here of the particular help he found. It carried him
to success as manager of New York's famous Astor
Hotel and guides him today as New York State
Boxing Commissioner.

THE DAY a fellow ships home after a war should be thrilling. But I was a frightened lad of 20 when a big transport pulled away from France in 1918. I wasn't facing forward. I hung over the ship's rail looking at the foreign shores. Somewhere there in France was my right arm.

I yearned to go home and crawl in a hole. But I knew I'd hate myself if I did it. Yet I just couldn't lather up any more *effort*. For a peace-loving people, we Americans have seen a lot of warring. It appears not unlikely that we'll see more. My share of war was over. But if ever I was scared stiff in battle, I was twice as scared at the thought of living and what was ahead.

Just as bad, if not worse than lacking a limb, was the realization that I was ignorant. Hauling me smack out of a quiet Southern town in my teens, the Army had whisked me through New York, over the Atlantic Ocean and a slice of Europe. In each mile of it I had felt more and more the intellectual barefoot boy.

When I arrived home I would be faced with the problem of how to find a job. Could a fellow really wise himself up, really enough to be part of a complicated world?

And supposing such a dream were impossible, how could I

* *Matthew 6: 3*

keep from being a semi-invalid? Could I live a full man's life?

All around me were men charged with the excitement of going home. Yet I knew most of them were as frightened inside as I was and as full of questions about an uncertain future.

When I went below to turn in early that first night on shipboard, I was jumpy. I dug through my kit until I found my own special sedative, the book my grandfather put into my hands the night before I went into service: his Bible.

As Grandpa had told me to, I had turned to it often, when home and plain living were an ache inside. I pored over it that night, with the ship's nose heading toward the States, and my home town of Milan, Tennessee. And I fell to remembering Grandpa. I could see my Grandfather, the minister of our town, standing straight, as he spoke the words of God. He had always been absurdly partial to me, probably because I was forever in a peck of trouble.

He died while I was overseas. When I opened his Book after that I told myself his hand had smoothed the pages and his eyes had traveled the words. The memory of him steadied me. That first night sailing home I'd have given most anything to be able to talk to him: "Grandpa, how do you lift the load with one hand?"

Back home, I found his answer everywhere. In his room, his chair, his church, his town. The memories he had left were messages of what he had stood for. The conviction grew that he had given me all the answers when he placed his Book in my hands.

And very deep those words of His penetrated my heart. What *had* I to fear? Paul's words have given courage and confidence to so many and they made me a man again: *"If God be for us, who can be against us?"**

One day when the sun rose, I stood up ready to live ... to take the first job that was offered me ... to get books and study so that

* *Romans 8: 31*

I might prepare for better and better jobs. I was no longer afraid. And not being afraid, I was no longer self-conscious. I forgot the empty sleeve and the missing arm. The less I thought of it, the less anyone noticed.

The day came when I got an offer of a job in Florida. Before I left I went up to Grandpa's study again. I remembered how many times I'd burst in on him when I was hurt or in trouble, knowing so well that he loved me enough to help, forgive, advise, and make me *want* to be somebody special. Often he said to me: "You have a Father in heaven who loves you more than I do, Bob boy. Never forget it, and learn to go to Him for anything, no matter how bad you've been."

It seemed like the last needed lesson to recall as I headed off to Florida to face the world of business and the urge to climb upward. From then on I've had no hesitancy to ask my heavenly Father for *anything,* large or small. Or to thank Him.

My prayers, most of which Grandpa had taught me, became as necessary as food. Mingling with others who were seeking to know God better was strengthening; church and Bible classes and spiritual discussions were nourishment, and lifting up my voice in the hymns of praise and love brought joy.

But best of all was *sharing* the faith that did so much for me. Passing it on. Proving it to people. Urging them to prove it to themselves.

One learns not to speak of it much. I seldom mention it at first to the many handicapped people who seem to seek me out to get a job. They've been told over and over again in their painful days about God. I am about the only kind of human being who can dare to be tough with them.

"I don't care *what's* the matter with you," I shrug, and wag my empty sleeve at them for emphasis. "You have a brain. Nothing wrong with your mind, is there? Those are the only people my heart aches for. As for *you,* how *good* are you? What can you do?

What have you got to contribute to the world? If you're competent, that's all that matters. And I'll give you a job or help you get one."

When delivered with a smile, there isn't one of them who doesn't sit up higher and smile back.

But there are times when it's called for to speak of faith.

I stopped in at my favorite haberdashery recently for a sweater I needed. The shop owner, who had been ailing, was quite plainly on the verge of collapse.

"Sam," I said. "What's wrong?"

"I'm a sick man, Mr. Christenberry." Then, unable to speak further, he lowered his face.

"Sam," I told him, "I'm going to send you to the Greatest Physician in the world, and right this minute. Your boy can do up my sweater."

The man lifted his eyes to mine.

"Down in the basement," I said quietly, "is your stock room. You go down there and talk to your God. Tell Him all your troubles and fears. Ask Him to help. After all, if He created you, He can take care of you. You stay down there in quiet, and listen to Him."

Two weeks later, a big box was on my desk. The card inside read: "A new hat for you, from a friend you made a new man of."

I stopped in his shop later to thank him. He *was* a new man. But I expected him to be. The help never fails for those who go to God with an earnest and seeking heart, "as a little child."

Am I not a walking proof?

Illustration, Bob Christenberry, see page 236

YOUR FAITH CAN
KNOCK OUT FEAR

by **GENE TUNNEY**

*When you think of Tunney, you think of his spec-
tacular victory over Jack Dempsey. This story re-
veals the fight before the fight . . . how Gene was
beaten before he ever got into the ring . . . and how
he found a way to bounce back to win boxing's most
famous championship battle.*

I WAS ONE scared young man on the morning of the New Year
in 1920. The opponent whom I was scheduled to box that afternoon was a tough veteran named Whitey Allen, as cagey and
experienced a fighter as they come.

It was one of my first bouts since returning from France where
I had served as a Marine in World War I. I was still wet behind
the ears in the professional fighting sense. My fear on this day was
based on a fear that I'd had all my life—of professionals.

I can remember praying that morning as fervently and
humbly as any man ever has. I prayed that in the fight that afternoon I might not be permanently injured when I was knocked
out. I didn't ask that I might win. I took it for granted that I'd
be knocked out, and I was terribly afraid of being hurt for life.

The prize ring is a rather terrifying place when you think
about it. You're up on a raised platform which is a glare of light.
All around you is the dim expanse of the crowd. You see faces
wrenched with expressions of frantic excitement, emotions produced by the lust for battle—gloating, savage mouths open with
yelling.

In every fighter comes occasionally the supreme horror of not
being able to fend off the blows showered on him, of being helpless to raise his hands to ward them off.

Thus when I prayed that I might not be permanently injured, I gained confidence that I wouldn't be. This took the edge off mad, irrational fear. If it hadn't been for this confidence I gained from prayer, I imagine that I'd have gone into the ring inwardly shaking and quaking, thoroughly beaten in advance.

As it was, I climbed into the ring that day with enough courage to go through the orthodox procedures of fighting a normal fight. In the second round I suddenly realized how groundless my fears had been. My opponent was no super-man. I went on to win the fight.

Thus I had scored one victory over fear. But years later faintness of heart nearly cheated me out of the championship.

This happened before my title bout with Jack Dempsey. Dempsey, the Manassa Mauler, was an overwhelming favorite to thump me out in an early round. Newspapers talked of what a murderous lacing he would give me. Being human I read the papers to find out what they were saying about me.

One night at the beginning of my long training period I awakened suddenly and felt my bed shaking. It seemed fantastic. Ghosts or what? Then I understood. It was I who was shaking, trembling so hard that I made the bed tremble. I was that much afraid—afraid of what Dempsey would do to me. The fear was lurking in the back of my mind and had set me quaking in my sleep, the nightmare thought of myself being beaten down by Dempsey's shattering punches.

The vision was of myself, bleeding, mauled and helpless, sinking to the canvas and being counted out. I couldn't stop trembling. Right there I had already lost that ring match which meant everything to me—the championship. I had lost it— unless I could regain it.

I got up and took stock of myself. What could I do about this terror? I could guess the cause. I had been thinking about the fight in the wrong way. I had been reading the newspapers, and all they had said was how Tunney would lose. Through the newspapers I was losing the battle in my own mind.

Part of the solution was obvious. Stop reading the papers. Stop thinking of the Dempsey menace, Jack's killing punch and ferocity of attack. I simply had to close the doors of my mind to destructive thoughts—and divert my thinking to other things. It took discipline. And again prayer and faith were pillars of strength to me.

This was the right medicine since I did go out and beat Dempsey in two straight fights. And the one moment when I was closest to defeat—I had been knocked to the canvas for a count of nine—produced the most humorous touch. Father Francis Duffy, the great World War I chaplain of the Fighting Sixtyninth, and a close friend of mine, was at the fight. Sitting behind him was a very demonstrative young man. When I was lying dazed on the canvas, this young fellow went wild with excitement and noticing that Father Duffy, sitting in front of him, was a priest, pounded him violently on the back.

"Father, for Judas' sake, pray for Gene."

Father Duffy told me afterward that he instinctively began to pray, not that I would win over my opponent, of course, but that I would do my best and deliver to the fullest extent of my powers. That's the prayer of a sportsman.

I wonder how many millions of people face similar fears in their own lives. Not necessarily fears of physical nature either. Perhaps they too have been thinking too destructive thoughts.

A simple illustration is that of a man who is afraid of losing his job. He dwells on the imaginary scornful remarks his friends will make, the loss of face. Soon he visualizes a completely pitiful picture of himself. And it is more than likely in this case he will lose his job because of such negative thinking.

From my experience in two world wars I can also say that fear is the dominant emotion of a soldier. He fights his terror, dwells on it and it only increases. But how to get one's mind off fear? Religious fervor is a state of feeling like fear, and there are age-old exercises for stirring an ardor of faith.

The principal of these is prayer. You can pray away your terrors, if you have enough faith. You can become spiritually exalted instead of afraid. Religious emotion can take the place of fear.

I speak of the practical necessity of faith and prayer, because that's the part about which I know the most; I know it from experience. I speak as one to whom religious belief has been a lifelong resource—this in a life given so largely to a career of fighting. I know faith and prayer as creative forces for courage.

These personal experiences have made me value the belief, the traditional worship and the church in which I was reared. They also made me more hostile to the dark anti-religious forces that would destroy the happiness and the wonder of the faith of ages.

I recall a beautiful expression of John McCormack, the great lyric master of song. During my visit to Ireland I had an opportunity to see a great deal of him. His favorite expression, striking, characteristic, was a parting good-bye. "May God keep you in the palm of His hand," he would say with all the melody of an Irish brogue. In it was all the folklore flavor of Irish mysticism, that sense of intimacy of the Divine, enjoying the friendship of God. An expression too of simple faith in the goodly order of the universe.

Illustration, Gene Tunney, see page 237

MOM AND POP
WENT TO COLLEGE

by **BERTHA C. ROYAL**

> *Although Lillian and Owen Barnes had five chil-*
> *dren, they both decided to get a college education.*
> *Here is how they did it against seemingly insur-*
> *mountable obstacles.*

I'D LIKE TO TELL you about my neighbors, the Barneses. For four years I watched all seven of them go to school together—that's right, mother and father and their five children.

When Lillian and Owen Barnes decided to *start* college in 1949, they already had their five children. Lillian was 30 then; Owen was 31. They had been graduated together from the same high school in Canton, Ohio, 14 years earlier.

Then a few months after their graduation they were married. Owen, the son of a minister, turned to the serious business of supporting his family. Except for World War II service, he worked steadily in the steel mills and, on the side, earned a few extra dollars as a house painter and paper hanger.

Now we all like to learn, but few are willing to pay the price. I don't know anyone who would have paid the price Lillian and Owen Barnes did to satisfy their hunger for education and find a better place in the sun for their children.

They enrolled as freshmen at Kent University, 26 miles away. Every morning Lillian would pack seven lunches, and then she and her husband would walk a mile through the pre-dawn darkness to a point where a fellow student would pick them up in his car and drive them to the campus in time for their 8:00 a.m. classes. At 4:00 p.m. their student friend would deposit them at the pick-up point, from there they would walk the mile back home.

At the start of their sophomore year, they bought an ancient car for the 52 mile round trip from Canton to Kent and back. "We prayed for two things about that car," says Owen, "that it wouldn't break down and that somehow we'd have money to meet the payments."

After nine hours of school and travel, Lillian did her washing, ironing, cooking, and sewed clothes for her son Ronald, now 17, and her four daughters: Lora, 15; Judith, 14; Michaele, 11, and Jacqueline, 10. The children did most of the cleaning. When school was over, Owen went to work as a paper hanger—whenever there was work—and rarely got home before midnight. In his senior year at college he got a job at Republic Steel on the late-afternoon-to-midnight shift.

With classes and chores finished, and the children asleep, Owen and Lillian would sit down after midnight and concentrate on their studies.

For four years they averaged five hours sleep a night and often less. At times their nerves were so raw and ragged Owen would look at his wife and say, "It isn't worth it. Let's quit." And Lillian would smile a very tired smile and answer, "Let's go back just tomorrow."

So the next morning they would go back, probably stimulated by the exuberance of their children who loved the idea of Mom and Pop going to school, too. In this case, the Barnes youngsters made sacrifices so their parents could have a complete education.

"But we never neglected them," says Lillian firmly. "We would have quit at once if they had suffered. And they're all going to go to college, too. We'll see to that."

Owen had some help from the GI Bill of Rights, and Lillian from a full-tuition scholarship during her last three years. Yet, they often wonder how they managed to pay rent and buy food. For about a year Ronald and Lora, the two oldest children, worked after school. Their income wasn't much, but every pair of shoes they bought for themselves meant two pairs less their parents had to buy.

"Truly, it was a case of 'give us this day our daily bread,'"* says Lillian.

"If we had tried to figure it out on paper," Owen says, "we never would have started. I wouldn't advise anyone who wants to go to college to have five children first."

They never told their instructors, nor anyone at Kent, about their five children and certainly said nothing about their tribulations. They wanted no special consideration.

I had to laugh when Lillian told me how, as a freshman, she tried to get into a class in advanced English composition which was open only to juniors. Exceptions were made with the instructor's permission. So Lillian asked the instructor.

"Absolutely no!" he snapped. "Out of the question! I never allow freshmen in this class. They're too young and inexperienced and have nothing to write about."

Lillian planted herself firmly in his path: "I'm 30 years old," she said, "and I have had some experiences that would amaze you."

She got into the class.

The Barneses are active members of St. Paul's African Methodist Episcopal Church here in Canton. Lillian had sung in the choir from childhood and was often the soloist. During their school years, however, they could do little except worship there, and Lillian sang only special music at Easter and Christmas.

"Perhaps our trials were an important part of our education," says Owen, "because even from moments of despair came renewed faith."

They were graduated in June 1953. Lillian, one of the 59 honor students in a class of 600, got a Bachelor of Arts degree in psychology. Owen received a Bachelor of Science degree in business

* *Matthew 6: 11*

administration and was an honor student in his major subject.

Directly after graduation Lillian was hired to teach special classes in the Canton public schools. But, since her degree was in liberal arts, she needed 19 credits in education to qualify for her temporary teaching job. So she promptly returned to Kent that summer to earn them, attending classes six days a week and running her house as usual.

Other neighbors besides myself have been concerned over the Barneses. We couldn't help but wonder about the faith that kept them going.

"Our faith was not something that we dragged out and examined," Owen answered. "But it was always there. It never occurred to us for more than a few minutes at a time that we would not make it."

Owen has returned to Kent to work on his Master's degree and has been given a graduate assistantship in the Department of Business Administration, teaching one freshman class. He enjoys it so much he'll try to make teaching his life's work.

Their faith will never waiver because of what they are, and also because of a professor Lillian had at Kent. He was in the Philosophy Department; a learned, wise, God-conscious man. Lillian took every course in religion he gave, and much of what she learned filtered down to Owen and the children.

"Under his guidance," she says, "we have all grown in our awareness that all life and good emanate from God—'the Circle whose center is everywhere and whose circumference is nowhere.' At one time I might have repeated that by rote. But now I *know*."

And Owen corrects her gently, "Now we all *know*."

Illustration, the Barnes family, see page 236

THE CHILDREN'S POLICEMAN

by JAMES E. MITCHELL

Here's a policeman who keeps gum and safety pins in his pocket for children. They call him Uncle Mike—and he's an institution in Ware, Massachusetts.

I WAS DRIVING slowly through the town of Ware, Massachusetts recently, when a policeman suddenly signaled me to a halt.

"You're a stranger in town," the policeman said. "Is there anything I can do to help you?"

He showed me where to park, helped me to find my destination, then, while saying goodbye, he offered me a stick of gum.

Surprised, I asked about this friendly, unusual behavior. "That's Mike Houlihan," I was told. "He's a friend of just about everybody. Especially the children. Mike can't keep from being helpful; it's as much a part of him as his ruddy cheeks and sparkling blue eyes."

"Mike must have been a policeman here for many years to have so many friends," I said.

"Only seven, though he's lived in Ware all his sixty-eight years."

On my return to Ware, weeks later, I was greeted by Mike almost before I saw him. And by name. As we talked, every few words were interrupted by children: "Hi, Mike"; "Hello, Uncle Mike"; or "Hello, Mickey."

Then I saw Mike lean over for a short, intense conversation with a little girl of eight or nine. I overheard him say, "If you want to be a sweetheart of mine, you'll have to stay right up with the others." The child, with a tear glistening in her eyes, shook her head enthusiastically in assent. Mike patted her little shoulder, and she hurried off. He turned to me. "She failed her school lessons yesterday and she knew I'd hear about it. I always tell them that I know it when something has gone wrong, and they see it doesn't happen again."

Then he added, "It's a shame, but so many children today just don't get the affection at home they need."

Another little girl ran up to him, smiling. "Uncle Mike, will you pin this for me, please?" He dutifully reached in a pocket, pulled out a card of safety pins, took one, pinned her belt for her, and, as was his practice, gave her a piece of gum.

"I always carry pins," he told me. "You'd be surprised at how many need pinning up."

Further questioning brought out the information that Mike had once been a prosperous businessman in Ware. His career began at the age of twelve in a grocery store. The owner advised him to start his own business.

"If you work half as hard for yourself as you do for other people, Mike, you'll do well." Mike went into the restaurant business and proved the grocer right: he was highly successful.

Then the Houlihan's only son died a year after graduating from Holy Cross College. Mike felt, somehow, that he should have been able to prevent it.

For Mike life was no longer the same. He sold his business, idled his time away. Then Ware's now-retired Police Chief Buckley talked to him about going back to work as a policeman in this town of 9,000.

"Mike has a peculiar slant on things. He thinks everybody's all right. He thinks everyone wants to do the right thing. Once Mike saw he could do some good, especially with children, he was sold," says Chief Buckley. "He took to the job with a vengeance."

In his "spare time" Mike now runs Halloween parties, plays

Santa Claus, keeps the children in tow at the local theatre on Saturdays, and handles the municipal pool and playground during the summer. He visits every sick child in town—at home, or in the hospital.

When the pool was first built, some children used to have money stolen. When Mike went on duty, he told the youngsters to leave their change with him. They'd slip it into his "money" pocket, take it out when they left. Mike never touched the money himself, never knew how much the children put in or took out. Not once has the money come out wrong at the end of the day.

One day I asked Chief Buckley why Mike gave away so much gum.

Replied the Chief, "He told me once that he heard a child refuse gum to a friend. Mike figured he would at least wipe out that selfish trait."

I kept thinking about all the gum Mike gives away—nearly one hundred sticks a day. Then I wrote a letter. A reply came from Mr. E. H. James, of Beech-Nut, who said, in part:

" . . . we are well aware of, and very fond of, Officer Houlihan. If you were to ask this fine gentleman where he gets his gum, you would find that we supply it gratis. And we are mighty happy to do it. It is strange that heartbreaking personal experience seems to create bitterness in some individuals, but in others like Mike Houlihan it lights a bright light of kindness and generosity that shines for the rest of us . . ."

I learned later that, before he came to the attention of this company, Mike used to buy the gum himself. Chief Buckley says:

"Mike doesn't smoke or drink, so he felt that money he might have spent on these things could go for gum. I figure it used to cost him six or seven dollars a week."

When Mike offered me a stick later that day, I asked him if he ever ran out.

"I make allowance for such things," he replied with a twinkle. "I keep a few hundred sticks of gum on deposit in the bank here at the corner all the time."

"Mike," I asked, "what do you think is the most important thing in life?"

His face grew serious. "I haven't missed church more than three times in the past forty years," he said, "but when my boy died, part of me died too. I lost 60 pounds and really had the doctors worried. But if your belief in God goes deep, you don't give up. I found that out."

Mike can talk about his son now. But no one knows how many times he is thinking of his own boy while helping someone else's. There was the crippled youngster, Robert Sands. Mike visited him every day in the hospital. On his release, Mike regularly wheeled Robert to the playground, where he would tell the boy when to swim and when to sun himself. Tenderly the policeman's strong, supple fingers massaged the wasted limbs.

Then—and this must be Mike's real reward—the boy's mother came to Mike one day, with tear-brimmed eyes.

"The doctor came this morning, Mike," she said. "Little Robert will be all right in every way. Mr. Sands and I . . . well, you know what I want to say. Thanks, Mike."

Illustration, Mike Houlihan, see page 236